William J. Dolan

The 7 Disciplines of RELATIONSHIP MARKETING

The Greatest Marketing Plan in History and how you can harness it to transform your company, your culture and you.

William J. Dolan

Copyright

Cover design: Kelly Anderson, Willy Dolan, Zee Farrouge, Ricky Russ, Jr.

Editing: Anne DeRock, Todd Hunter
Audiobook Produced by Zee Farrouge at Spirit Media

Dedication

To my high school sweetheart, wife and business partner, Camilla, one of the most beautiful, committed, faithful, and patient people I have ever known.

Also, to my incredible family, Heather, Brittain, Killeen, William, Keenan, Christine, Oliver, Nibras, Chy and Chance. I love you with all my heart.

To my late father, who taught me how to work hard and fight.

Finally, to my mother, who taught me the value of education, persistence and how to make cookies. Each of those lessons changed my life.

William J. Dolan

Table of Contents

The 7 Disciplines of Relationship Marketing

Chapter 1

Why Most Marketing Sucks

*Behind all bad marketing
is a leader who asked for it.
- Anonymous*

Marketing, in general, is getting more complex, confusing and is much harder not easier. Given the complexity and difficulty of finding people who can master strategy, tactics and the ever-changing marketing landscape leads to one tragic scenario; most marketing sucks. Oh, I know. The rest of the world wants to tell you differently, in part, because so many are selling quick fixes or silver bullets. Not to say that there aren't legitimate marketers out there, but too many so-called experts are like snake oil salesman trying to sell the illusion that doing just one thing will fix everything. I'm afraid I know that pitch all too well. When I started my career in television, the sales department did a brilliant job of convincing businesses that all their sales and marketing woes would be cured with a TV commercial. Unfortunately, it wasn't true then and it isn't true now.

---

*Marketing silver bullets
simply do not exist.*

What About Your People?

Finding great people who really are great at marketing is crazy tough. Like a lot of organizations, we trust that our teams are working from the right strategies, producing brilliant creative and executing with surgical precision. But that's usually not the case. It's not that our marketing teams are not busy. They are very busy but often working on projects that can only produce modest results. They, like so many marketers, are driven by trends and the fear of missing out. They try one thing, and then another because someone told them that they were bad marketers if they didn't do it. And you, in an attempt to improve outcomes, may be guilty of suggesting that they try something you might have seen somewhere, but that typically doesn't help. Inevitably, your marketing team is conflicted between pleasing the customer and pleasing you. Guess what? No one is pleased. Finding the right people who have a foundational mastery of marketing (we call them rock stars) are few and far between.

How's Your Brand Doing?

Can we talk about your brand? Sadly, while every organization wishes that everyone would know and trust their brand, most brands, perhaps yours too, is weak to fair at best. It's true that the marketing team thinks it's crystal clear and everywhere because they just ordered new logoed jackets. Funny, that's what the folks at Radio Shack thought. But outside the safe confines of the offices, most brands are stale and about as clear and distinguishable as a wet plush toy.

Is Your Sales Team Making Their Numbers?

And how about the sales team? What's often unspoken is the intellectual mutiny that festered because the team doesn't really trust marketing to do anything of significance in the area of lead generation or sales enablement. The team has pretty much determined that they are on their own. Their best plan, if they actually want to make a dent in top line revenues, is to just hope and hustle. Deep down, we all know that a long-term strategy based on the sales team (or sales channels) leading the way to the promised land, ultimately results in underperformance, burnout and turnover. Oh wait. Are you the sales team?

Tragically, I see this every day and if this sounds a bit like you, you're not alone. It's just the world we live in and one that is often modeled over and over. The hardest part is how much it is costing your organization in valuable time, wasted money and the pain that is inflicted on a culture that does not see vibrant growth but instead feels stagnation and frustration.

Relationship Marketing is What People Want

The great news is that it doesn't have to be this way. For thousands of years, faith, philosophy and the arts have offered intriguing models about what drives human behavior. For more than a century, great business schools have refined curriculums to better provide a comprehensive understanding of business and marketing.

In the last couple decades, technological breakthroughs have opened doors to more efficient ways to connect with markets and better measure outcomes. And most recently, 21st Century companies have broken new ground and revealed the power of customer-driven innovation. But perhaps most exciting, is the more recent embrace and implementation of relationship marketing, simply one of the most powerful practices to drive great marketing and world-class brands. In 1999, Zappos was born with the goal of embodying a relationship culture by striving to offer the very best service and selection to its customers. What really stood out for Zappos was that the company made the same level of commitment to its employees. This 360-degree relationship model not only positioned Zappos to be acquired in 2009 by Amazon but has led to teaching the *Delivering Happiness* model, based on the bestselling book by Tony Hsieh, to organizations around the world. The experience and science that supports this model is impressive and can literally transform an organization from the inside out.

Imagine your organization with a thriving and growing marketing system. Can you picture the confidence your people would have if they came to work lifted by an inspiring purpose and vision? What if you had absolute confidence that you were talking to all the right markets in all the right ways? Imagine your customers, vendors, and the community acting like a glowing chorus of voices singing your praises, sending you leads and building your brand. What if you knew that you were investing in the people and campaigns that would bring you the highest return on investment over and over? Picture having a metrics dashboard, like the dashboard in your car that would allow you to steer or accelerate your marketing vehicle to the destinations of your choosing. And how sweet would it be if your marketing system acted like a flywheel that could continue to spin with the power of shear purposeful momentum.

Now I understand what you might be thinking; *This can't be true and if it is, it will cost too much, or it will take forever.* That is a natural response but thankfully, one that you really shouldn't fear. In fact, applying this strategic framework could actually save you time and money. The bottom line is that the strategy works and the fact that you are reading *The 7 Disciplines of Relationship Marketing* is the first powerful step. And the next step will be sharing and implementing the disciplines within your organization.

The principles are time-tested and proven with both historic and contemporary case studies. Best of all, they operate within the natural heart of the human relationship experience. This strategy will beautifully drive down to the core of who you are, what your organization is all about and will help you live and operate in integrity. Your organization will come to appreciate that great marketing is not about tactics or manipulation, but about telling the truth, exceptionally well.

Now, I'd love to tell you that *The 7 Disciplines of Relationship Marketing* (the 7DRM Strategy) was the product of my natural creativity and brilliance but I'd be lying. Despite the fact that I have been working in the field of television, entertainment and marketing for over 30 years, the truth is that it was something that I discovered. These are powerful disciplines that have been around for centuries and it is very likely that they have played a part in your life, right in front of you, for years. Sometimes it takes a two-by-four to get my attention and that really worked this time. I wish I could say that my discovery was a product of attending an enlightening class or reading a good book. Instead, it was my death. Yes, I actually died and had a life-altering death experience that allowed me to open my eyes to the 7DRM Strategy. It was this experience that truly changed my life and led me on one of the greatest adventures I could ever hope for. My prayer is that it can change you too and it is my honor and privilege to share it with you now.

Chapter 2

The Day I Died
Changed Everything

It is worthy dying to find out what life is.
T.S. Elliot

I grew up in a blue-collar neighborhood in Portland, Oregon. As the only child of a classic Irish-Catholic family, I followed tradition; obey your parents, go to catholic school, work hard, learn to box, and eat a lot of meat and potatoes. My mom took some time away from her nursing career to be home with me while my dad worked as a meat cutter. Those times as a young boy with my Mom were precious as she would play the piano with me and teach me to bake, two skills I still practice today. Along the way, the nuns at the convent thought I had a gift and trained me in classical piano. I did have a go at violin, but my father couldn't stand to hear me practice so he made me quit.

Up until third grade, my life was pretty sweet, that was, until my father became ill. My mom went back to working the night shift at the hospital while my dad and I stayed home. Those nights alone were tough, but I found escapes, sometimes with Maureen, the widow across the street who would lecture me on art, design, fashion and God. The rest of the time, this was before the rise of video games, you could find me immersed in the refuge of the television screen absorbing the romance, drama and horror of classic movies. My mother, father, Maureen and movies helped shape the trajectory of my life while influencing what later would become my career.

Launching a Career

In high school, I was interested in speech and language, but TV and entertainment really excited me. After volunteering as the weekend DJ at a local college (interestingly, the one Steve Jobs was attending), I was totally hooked on media and started my formal education as a television production major. From there, my life launched into high gear. At 20, while still in college, I was hired by the local ABC affiliate station and became one of the youngest major market directors in the country. At 22,

I married my beautiful high school sweetheart. At 25, I started a side business and what would eventually become our creative agency, Spirit Media. My life was an exciting mix of directing live television programs, working side-by-side with local and national agencies developing commercials, and then producing live corporate events on nights and weekends. My wife and I became the proud parents of four incredible kids but by 32, after having directed over 10,000 promos, commercials and full-length programs, I was exhausted and left the TV station. Both terrified and thrilled, for the first time, I had to learn how to support my family solely as the owner of an independent creative agency.

Stepping Out in Faith

To put it simply, my entry into entrepreneurship left me both stretched and blessed. Doors opened all around the country as I had developed a solid resume around television directing, video production, experiential events and marketing. I directed projects with everyone from Alec Baldwin and Arnold Schwarzenegger to Bill O'Reilly and President Bill Clinton. There is another book around those experiences. I found myself connecting well with the music/entertainment space and directing shows with some of the most popular Christian bands as well as global rock stars like Maroon 5, Black Eyed Peas and Gwen Stefani. Whether working with entertainers, world leaders or rock stars, you get a powerful sense of what high stakes branding is all about. It demands that you perform at an extremely high level. Every detail has to be meticulously monitored and managed because they are all the living embodiments of their brands. One slip up and a brand is immediately compromised and must be rebuilt before it can rise to be at its most effective again, if ever. When a single person or entity, like a rock band, is the centerpiece of the brand, attention to details are the difference between fair, good and an excellent reputation. This should be a particular caution to any business owner or leader.

Your reputation powerfully impacts the quality of your brand.

Equally fascinating was working with global brands like Intel, Nike, Adidas and Microsoft. Working side by side with their PR teams, marketing managers and product developers really opened my eyes to how strategic these giants must be to grow and manage their brands. Between the matrix of products, demographics, advertising, public relations, marketing, constant research and development, these machines were humming with the competitive intensity of a freight train. Like the entertainment world, their attention to detail was critical but with a giant magnifying glass focused on one big thing-shareholder value. As public companies, they had to keep their shareholders happy and that meant good forecasts, earnings reports and rising stock prices. *One of the biggest lessons from these clients was the need to be exceptionally strategic, creative and deliver flawless execution.*

Through most of my career, I was learning a lot and having a ball. The money was good and to be completely honest, my head was getting pretty big. I even had the chance to fund and produce my first full-length documentary while my wife and I had our fifth child. To my delight, the documentary project was well received, and we agreed to terms with a national distributor. All I had to do was fly to Nashville to sign the contracts and collect our advance check. Could it get any better?

Death: My New Beginning

On a crisp January morning, the kind where, as you depart from Portland International Airport, you are greeted by one of the most beautiful and iconic views of the Pacific Northwest, the majestic Mt. Hood. This time of year, at over 11,000 feet, it is covered in a rich blanket of snow that makes you feel fortunate to live in this part of the world. I was flying to Nashville with one of my best friends in the world, Timothy Greenidge. Timothy is the kind of guy that just makes you smile. Not only is he one of the greatest gospel singers in the world, he is a highly sought-after music producer and audio engineer. We had worked several shows around the country together and as a tall black man with the strength and build of a professional football player, he was quite the contrast to my pale lepriconish frame.

Multiple times every month, I was on a plane flying somewhere, but this flight seemed different.

Multiple times every month, I was on a plane flying somewhere, but this flight seemed different. I forgot that this particular day was the seventh anniversary of the day that I started my new life when I walked out of the TV station. You'd think that something that was so life-changing for me would be on my mind. Instead, I was thinking about how strange I felt. I couldn't put my finger on it, but I was feeling sick. *Oh no, not sick, not today, not here!* I became light-headed and I thought I might pass out. I turned to Timothy and all I could say was, *Something isn't right!* That's the last thing I said before my eyes rolled back in my head. My arms fell limp by my side and my heart stopped. At first, Timothy thought I might be joking but he quickly realized that something was seriously wrong. He didn't know formal CPR, but he knew about chest compressions and he urgently began administering his best version right there in my seat. When I didn't respond, he pulled me to the center aisle and was about to break my ribs when suddenly, I started to breathe again.

Needless to say, the scene of my lifeless body and Timothy working to save my life prompted an in-flight medical emergency and an immediate landing. Over the next few weeks, and a confirmation from the cardiac team in Portland, I was diagnosed with malignant neurocardiogenic syncope. In short, my brain and heart get confused and my brain tells my heart to stop and you die. Doctors don't know what causes it but the best way to treat it is to implant a pacemaker. That way, my pacemaker can monitor my heart rate and if, for any reason, it makes a sudden drop, I can be paced to a normal rhythm and avoid collapsing to my death. Even as I write this book, my pacemaker intervenes an average of six times a day and as long as the battery holds, I'll be able to finish this book for you. If all the pages are here, you know I made it.

> *The most amazing thing about the entire experience is that I remember everything.*

The most amazing thing about the entire experience is that I remember everything. No, it wasn't one of those floating over my body looking at myself experiences. It was one where as my eyes rolled back into my head and any vision of this dimension of time and space drifted away, I immediately crossed a threshold into eternity.

The peace was consuming, and I felt as if a light, like a laser beam, pierced the top of my head and I was infused with a sense of understanding.

I just got it. As if finally finding the key to a puzzle you have been trying to solve all your life, everything made such simple yet profound sense. But nothing was more overwhelming and humbling as when I came face-to-face with God.

The Discovery

There is so much more to the experience that I'll share later in the book. All I will say now is that it profoundly changed me. And if a person weren't a little spiritual or religious before something like this, you certainly get really curious and start doing some deep exploration. I began looking at things differently as I tried to grasp what I had experienced. I questioned what I was doing with my life. I questioned if I was doing things the right way. I questioned why I was given my life back. With the assistance of a fascinating compilation of the gospels called *Jesus Christ, the Greatest Life*, I began studying the life of Jesus Christ. I was hungry to learn everything about what Jesus said and did. I wanted to understand what he taught, how he taught and why could this Jesus have made such a profound impact on this world in such a short time.

Now let me be clear that I am not a theologian. I am simply a husband, father and businessman who has spent the majority of my life swirling in the middle of this crazy media marketing machine. But what jumped off the pages absolutely blew me away!

> *With a level of clarity I had never experienced, it struck me that virtually every move Jesus made was incredibly strategic.*

With a level of clarity I had never experienced, it struck me that virtually every move Jesus made was incredibly strategic. He was no longer some mythical being or a caricature painted by his followers and critics. This was a man and a spiritual being, which I believe we all are, who functioned just like you and me in this world. Yes, he performed miracles, but the vast majority of his life was living, sleeping, breathing, eating, going to the bathroom, laughing, washing, talking, feeling, loving, making a living, launching a legacy and dying.

What I am saying is that he didn't just change the world with the wave of his hand. He came as a man in the flesh who operated with real people, with real messages, with real followers and enemies, and used a variety of methods to communicate his message. He faced an incredible backlash from the religious leaders of his time, and he was considered a disruption and threat to the Roman empire. Yet, he prevailed at launching the greatest and most lasting movement in history.

What he did, why he did it, where he did it, when he did it, to whom he spoke, with whom he associated, and the practices he modeled were nothing short of brilliant. I would conclude with absolute certainty that he modeled the greatest marketing strategy in the history of the world.

You can incorporate this marketing model into your organization today.

What may seem ironic is that the organizations that are flourishing by practicing elements of the Jesus model are companies like Amazon, Apple, and Lady Gaga! Whether they know it or not, their enterprises are thriving because they have put the Jesus model, the 7DRM Strategy to a significant level, into practice. But you know what's really exciting? You can incorporate this marketing model into your organization today.

As we move through *The 7 Disciplines of Relationship Marketing* and the 7DRM Strategy, I'll not only share the principles and some tools to help you start applying them, but I'll share one of our first campaigns using the strategy. I'll introduce you to the story of Paradise Point and how we used the 7DRM Strategy to transform an obscure Hawaiian home into an internationally known celebrity destination that was seen by millions around the world. When you hear what ultimately happened, I think you will be as blown away as we were at the journey.

Now, are you ready to learn the 7DRM Strategy and how it can transform your organization?

Chapter 3

The Secret is
Right in Front of You

*Your diamonds are not in far distant mountains or
in yonder seas; they are in your own backyard,
if you but dig for them.*

Russell H. Conwell

Light is an amazing thing. As someone who has invested decades learning the physics of light and how it impacts a scene, I love how it can illuminate the gentle contours of the human face and how, with just the right angles, it can highlight that gentle sparkle in a person's eyes. But light alone doesn't contain all the magic. For example, whenever you see those beautiful images of the earth or the moon floating in space, they seem to glow against the darkness of space. But wait. Is the earth glowing and is space really dark? Not really. Space is actually filled with massive amounts of radiant light. The earth, other than fires and street lights really has no natural glow. But what we witness is the beautiful relationship between light and an object when they touch. Only in that reflected moment do our eyes perceive the wonder of light as it illuminates an object. No, you didn't actually pick up a copy of *Cosmos*. I'm sharing this because it's the way love works. I can say, God loves, I love, or you love, but love, like light, is only revealed when there is an object of that love. That's why we say God loves you, or I love you, or you love me (thanks, I appreciate that). Despite the thousands of writings, poetry and songs that elevated it as some magical force, love only realizes the magic when it is expressed and experienced in relationship.

Yes, I Love You

Since my death, I want to make sure that no one ever questions my love for them. I say I love you often because I genuinely mean it. Now if the idea of love in business is too strong a term for you, we could say caring, serving, knowing, hearing, honoring, encouraging as these are all expressions of love or loving relationships. And isn't that at the core of what we all really want and need, to love and be loved? So why do we think that any organization can or should try to get away with simply conducting a transaction with a client versus having a meaningful relationship with a client? Wouldn't it be nice if a client felt us hearing them and looking them in their eyes instead of staring at their wallets? I'm talking figuratively here. That would be creepy. This is why we talk about the power of relationship marketing. Relationships are part of our wiring, our DNA and truly one of the most rewarding aspects of life. It is at the core of growing powerful, lasting organizations and it's always been right in front of you.

Mixed with all the beauty and wonder of a Hallmark movie comes the tragic prospect of a scene from the film Fatal Attraction.

But let's have a reality check here. Relationships are hard. Mixed with all the beauty and wonder of a Hallmark movie comes the tragic prospect of a scene from the film *Fatal Attraction*. There's a reason why there are breakups, strained relationships, business splits and even murders. People have different expectations and when those expectations aren't met, people get hurt and we move apart or retaliate which is always an unwise response. That is why it is essential to be very deliberate about developing, growing and retaining relationships. Just to show how deliberate you can be, check out the research from former Special Agent for the FBI, Dr. Jack Schafer.

In his book, *The Like Switch*, he reveals that the same strategies for profiling a terrorist can be used to turn a complete stranger into your friend. The first strategy is to create proximity, that is, get close. For example, can you think of any real friends in your life with which the awareness of that person didn't start out with being near them somehow? The next is frequency, in that the relationship has a chance to grow if encounters are more frequent. Curiously, frequency is an important marketing metric. The next is duration, in that your relationship results in engagements of greater duration. The last is intimacy. To what degree do the encounters move beyond simple surface level formalities? The only elements I would add to this formula for forming relationships are service, responsiveness and shared missions or goals. With this powerful formula, you begin to engage people at the place where relationships spark and flourish.

It's All in Your Head

While transactions, the simple act of exchanging money for goods or services is a necessary part of doing business, these pure transactions are believed to be a function of the frontal left side of the brain, known as the logical region. While we'd like to think that we are first, logical beings, many scientists will disagree. What we witness is that people are first, emotional beings in that we feel first, then run each experience through a complex journey of chemicals and electrical signals. This is where we feel the many forms of love. If it's romantic love, it's common for a potent concoction of chemicals to surge producing a feeling of euphoria or falling in love.

When you are in love,
you are really high as a kite.

Yes, when you are in love, you are really high as a kite. If it's more like the love you might develop for a brand, it's usually a consequence of similar chemicals being released over less intense but multiple exposures to cement the feelings of brand love or like. In either case, once these chemicals are released from the limbic system, we then translate those feelings as best we can into conscious words. In short, we make most buying decisions with our feelings and then justify them with our thoughts and words.

Time to Get Relactional

Relactional is a hybrid-concept illustrated by my mentor/friend, Ford Taylor in his book, *Relactional Leadership*. We see that most business engagements, whether inside or outside your organization, are a function of conducting transactions within the framework of genuine relationship. For this reason, we need to become conscientiously *Relactional*. Advertising guru, Roy Williams also encourages organizations to be deliberate about emphasizing relationship marketing. He notes that buyers in transactional shopping mode are more willing to spend time than money. But a buyer in relational shopping mode is more willing to spend money than time. Customers in relationship go right to the business that they like, know and trust. These customers are also historically, the source of about 80 percent of all gross profits.

Introducing the 7DRM Strategy

It is within this understanding that we now can grasp the power of relationship marketing and the 7DRM Strategy. It's important to point out that I don't believe that the 7 Disciplines are like a set of 10 Commandments. But I do believe that practicing the 7 Disciplines is like unlocking our own DNA and honoring the most deep and shared desires of every human being. They are so natural, honorable and effective at establishing and maintaining lasting relationships. It's no wonder why you see some of the most successful brands in the world like Amazon, Apple, Facebook, Google and Starbucks applying these principles at virtually every aspect of customer engagement. Best of all, with some education and a little coaching, you can begin to apply them to your organization now. Let me introduce them to you.

Mission

This is the first and the critical foundation to the success of any organization. Have you ever watched a skyscraper being built? It's exciting to watch as each floor rises above the landscape to form an iconic structure. The part that doesn't get a lot of fanfare is the foundation.

Depending on how grand the structure, the foundation and how deep you dig to form that foundation determines if the structure is sound.

Depending on how grand the structure, the foundation and how deep you dig to form that foundation determines if the structure is sound. Sadly, too many organizations skip this step or do a shallow exercise to draft some statement they can hang on the wall or publish in the employee handbook. You may be a little surprised at what it takes to honor the discipline of mission as we introduce you to your **Authentic Purpose Compass** and your *brand constitution* to help you establish a more robust foundation.

Market 2

This second discipline will help you focus on the very best markets for your organization. Here, we won't just address who will buy from you but reveal a powerful principle from the life of Jesus that will help you target with absolute confidence and purpose. We will also introduce you to the **10-Digit Human Address** that will help you to identify and reach your markets consistently and relevantly.

Message 3

In this third discipline, we will address one of the most difficult aspects of marketing. You think going on a first date is awkward? You should read the garbage that some people are writing in their marketing materials. In this chapter, we will introduce you to the **Message Matrix**, the ultimate message recipe for uncovering your messages to engage your markets along their buying journey. You won't be guessing anymore. You will know with confidence that you are saying the right things.

4 Messengers

In this fourth discipline, we discuss the power of messengers in not only delivering but amplifying your message. Whether you call them messengers, influencers, ambassadors or multipliers, this discipline is critical to building a vibrant organization. Most people have heard of CRM – Customer Relationship Management. In this chapter, we will discuss ARM – ***Ambassador Relationship Management,*** a key for leveraging the 7DRM Strategy.

5 Methods

In this fifth discipline, you'll learn the strategy for determining the best methods or tactics to support your business. It's fascinating that when most people talk about marketing, they want to jump to tactics but there is a very powerful reason why this is fifth discipline. In this chapter, we will address the strategic use of marketing tactics to remove obstacles, accelerate your buyer journey and increase profitability. We will also reveal the most terrifying red flag that every organization should avoid.

Measure 6

In this sixth discipline, we will not only address the power of metrics but introduce some best practices in business and marketing measurement. In this chapter, you'll discover one of the most powerful resources for constant improvement by reviewing your most important strategic, tactical and key performance indicators. We will outline the differences between lead and lag indicators to make sure that your teams are looking at the right dashboard.

Multiply 7

In this seventh discipline, you'll learn the secret of multiplication and how it can be the framework that connects and supports every aspect of your marketing plan. Ever change gears on a ten-speed bike? We will show you how to use the power of your marketing energy in a way that will multiply your marketing momentum to get you where you want to go faster and more efficiently.

Living in the world of media and marketing exposed me to the classic 4 P's of marketing; product, place, price and promotion. These are still very practical, but the

7DRM Strategy, when applied, is explosive. Like nitroglycerin, they are made up of some familiar compounds, but combined together, you have something extremely powerful. And you can apply the 7DRM Strategy to projects, campaigns or to your entire organization. They simply work!

But one last thing before we officially launch. Are you sure you are really prepared? Let's find out.

Chapter 4

You've Never Been More Ready

Good fortune often happens when opportunity meets with preparation.
Thomas A. Edison

While many will marvel at the greatest accomplishments in human history, most people forget in that moment of celebration and wonder, at the height of accomplishment, behind the victory is a season of preparation. The root of the word preparation (from Latin praeparatio) essentially means to get ready. Just like in a race, you find your mark, get ready and then go. We frequently get that out of order but there is power and opportunity for those who find their mark and then commit to getting ready.

Getting Ready

Few people consider that before Steve Jobs started Apple, he was a 14-year-old intern at Hewlett-Packard. Before Lady Gaga was a breakthrough star with the launch of her first album at 22, she was singing at open mics in New York as a teenager refining her craft and finding her audience.

The Preparation of Jesus

Jesus was no different. While stories of his childhood are thin at best, Jewish tradition, culture and archaeological records reveal what kind of upbringing this young man had and what may have shaped him into becoming such a powerful leader and world changer. Consider the fact that Jesus wasn't just a rabbi but was also being trained as a craftsman by his carpenter father, Joseph. It was common that rabbis also had a craft. Some would say that Jesus was more likely a practicing stonemason based upon the nature of the architecture in his part of the world. Regardless, the years leading up to his public launch at age 30 had the ingredients that prepared him to change the world. Consider the time. It's generally accepted that Jesus was born in 4 B.C, a time of incredible tension and conflict. The culture of Galilee was predominantly Jewish but was heavily influenced by the occupying Roman Empire. That region also sits at the intersection of some of the greatest historic powers. When we trace some of the trade routes and consider the economic influences from Egypt, Greece, the Persian Empire and the Roman Empire, Galilee was at the center in many ways of trade and commerce. This is the world that Jesus is born into.

If you follow the biblical narrative, Jesus is born in Bethlehem but then his family departs to Egypt to escape from Herod who is killing all the infant male children, known as the "Massacre of Innocents." Shortly thereafter, Herod the Great dies and Joseph is now going to return to his homeland. Nazareth is not only his home, but it also sits near one of the greatest building projects of his generation. Three miles from Nazareth, the shining model of Roman superiority in art, philosophy and wealth, the city of Sepphoris is being restored to the height of commercial glory. Antipas, the great son of Herod, has determined to fill the city with homes, a market place, a grand theatre, all in the rich tradition of high-end Roman art and architecture.

Contrary to the traditional depiction of Jesus as a secluded young boy in a rural setting, it's more likely that Jesus was mentored in a global urban landscape.

It was traditional for a Jewish child, who's studying to be a rabbi, to start studying the scriptures at age 5. Jesus had to learn scripture by memorizing passages. Households did not have the luxury of books but instead would reference scrolls in the synagogue or hear the scriptures recited orally. Young students would memorize them in both song and in chant. When not studying scripture, being the son of a craftsman, this was also the time for Jesus to learn a trade. Contrary to the traditional depiction of Jesus as a secluded young boy in a rural setting, it's more likely that Jesus was mentored in a global urban landscape with his father in the city of Sepphoris, considered the Shanghai of its time. This is where he was being prepared for his apprenticeships as a young tradesman. This also gave him exposure at a young age to multiple cultures and languages.

By age 12, Jesus made one documented appearance during the Passover feast in the temple. Even though it doesn't say much, the Greek author Luke, reveals how this young man was so smart that people marveled at his questions and teachings. In Jerusalem during the time of the Passover, given all the people who come to that area, this 12-year-old was so marvelous that people made note of him. Jesus had made an impression. Following Jewish tradition, Jesus at 13, entered the age of manhood where he would be held at a higher standard and accountable for his thoughts and actions. That's when he would intensify his focus on learning the family trade.

Craftsmen, like Jesus, were building major projects like homes, large public buildings, theaters and crafting beautiful art.

Archaeological digs have revealed much about the area. Jesus wasn't working in a hut making tables and chairs. Craftsmen, like Jesus, were building major projects like homes, large public buildings, theaters and crafting beautiful art. The work associated with Sepphoris was stunning and advanced for its day. This meant that Jesus was not only involved in significant building projects, he had to interact with a broad group of cultures. It could easily be presumed that by the time Jesus was 14, and a young apprentice, he could converse in a minimum of three to five languages. Jesus was not just a handy kid with a hammer who studied the scriptures. This was a young man who was growing in influence. He probably led construction crews on behalf of his father and was essentially conducting international business. When Jesus made his first big public appearance at age 30, he probably wasn't invited to the wedding in Cana simply because he was a nice guy. He was likely an esteemed rabbi and respected international businessman.

He probably led construction crews on behalf of his father and was essentially conducting international business.

Preparation for Mastery

Malcolm Gladwell wrote in the book, *Outliers*, about the 10,000 hours to mastery observation. He concludes that people who commit a minimum of 10,000 hours to their craft are more likely to achieve a level of world-class performance. While some find this hopeful, others find it discouraging because they feel that they will miss the window of opportunity. That is definitely a risk if your dream is to become a professional athlete. For example, we know that Tiger Woods started playing golf as a toddler and Serena Williams was hitting tennis balls in grade school.

> *We have a chance to build and open our own window of opportunity.*

But for many of us who are not dreaming about becoming professional athletes, we have a chance to build and open our own window of opportunity. For example, if money were the ultimate measure of success, we could say that Warren Buffett and Bill Gates hit their peak of accomplishment years ago. However, starting well past their 50s, both men committed themselves to leveraging their resources and influence to impact the world through humanitarian efforts. Their season of preparation for this level of accomplishment was a lot longer than that of most professional athletes. Similarly, Einstein worked for the better part of his entire career stumbling between hope and disappointment. This led to one of the most beautiful theories in history, the theory of relativity which changed the world.

What about you? How will you change the world? If the task seems daunting and you question if you should even continue reading this book, consider this; everything you have experienced in your life until today does not have to be just the passing of time but instead can be a platform for greatness. Regardless of the mistakes you may have made or the idea that you didn't move as fast as your peers or kept up with your expectations, today can be your launch day.

---

*Everything you have experienced in your
life until today does not have to be just
the passing of time, but instead can be a
platform for greatness.*

You've Never Been More Prepared Than Now

Given your life experience, you have never been wiser. You have never had more context about who you are and what you can bring to this world. You don't have all the answers, but you have a great perspective on things that don't work, and a book of life lessons learned from failure. You have already started your own season of preparation. You may be at a point where you are ready to launch into something life changing or where you need to get some refinement and clarity to take that dream to the next level and beyond. This book will help you validate or discover the compass that can point you in the direction of your authentic purpose. Now take a breath. Pause…do you hear that quiet? That's the sound after the launch pad has been built. By contrast, the countdown seems like a whisper. But it's counting for you. Let's get started.

Chapter 5

Building Your Launchpad

Average companies give their people something to work on. In contrast, the most innovative organizations give their people something to work toward.

Simon Sinek

After four months of reflection, discussion and prayer, on September 17, 1787, a group of visionary leaders established their first governing document, the Constitution of the United States. With an average age of 44, these writers shaped a document that lives and breathes today. It still is challenged, argued and honored but within it shows the classic model of what being missional is really all about.

In the same way, applying the discipline of mission and being missional is not something that can usually be constructed at a weekend retreat or half-day workshop. Let me just be blunt. The discipline of mission may be one of the hardest things you do for your organization. But getting it right may be one of the greatest things you ever do for your organization. For example, look at these missional declarations. All four are a part of global movements but one also was a death sentence.

Our vision is to be earth's most customer-centric company; to build a place where people can come to find and discover anything they might want to buy online.

Jeff Bezos, Amazon

To inspire and nurture the human spirit — one person, one cup and one neighborhood at a time.

Howard Schultz, Starbucks

To make a contribution to the world by making tools for the mind that advance humankind.

Steve Jobs, Apple

> *To proclaim good news to the*
> *poor…proclaim freedom for the prisoners*
> *and recovery of sight for the blind. To set*
> *the oppressed free to reclaim the year of*
> *the Lord's favor.*
>
> *Jesus Christ*

First Things First

When you think about building a great organization or creating a marketing plan, whatever it is, most people want to jump to the mechanics of it; *Let's do it. Let's put this activity together. Let's put this piece together.* But if you're doing something significant or something so powerful that it's going to have a lasting impact, then it's more like building a skyscraper. The building should go up after the foundation is deep and strong. Otherwise the building, like your organization, can be prone to swaying with the winds of adversity and change. Or, like what we have experienced on the west coast, some buildings need to be reinforced because they were never built strong enough to withstand powerful earthquakes.

Mission Manifesto

Whether you are building or reinforcing your organization, you have to know why you are doing it and what it's going to take to get it done. Asking those questions are critical and it applies whether you are doing something for you, your family, or if you're building an exceptional organization. The discipline of mission is more than a mission statement. It actually incorporates five major components to frame up your firm foundation. I call it your *Mission Manifesto*.

Purpose

The first part is purpose and it gets to the very core of our existence. It begs the question, Why am I here? That's not an easy question. In fact, it's one of the reasons why most people jump over it and get to *Let's get this party started*! instead of really digging into the deep hard work of asking *Why am I here*? Remember our framers of the constitution? They stated their *Why*, their purpose for even establishing a country, in the very first line of the constitution; *in Order to form a more perfect Union*. This statement became the foundation from which the rest of the constitution was constructed.

I work daily with diverse organizations who need to apply this discipline to projects and campaigns. Most organizations simply want me to draw them a map or just tell them what to do next. It reminds me of how we often approach life or our organizational missions. The unfortunate, but beautiful reality is, while most of us are praying to God to give us a map, God usually answers with a compass. This is both exciting and frustrating because instead of telling you every little thing that you need to do, it forces us to evaluate. It forces us to do introspection. It forces us to really think through the process and co-author the chapters of our lives together with God.

> *While most of us are praying to God to give us a map, God usually answers with a compass.*

The Authentic Purpose Compass

I like to use a tool I call the *Authentic Purpose Compass*. Think about it like a triangle with each point of the triangle representing a key to understanding your purpose. The first piece of that triangle is Passion. You've heard people say, *Just find your passion and you won't have to work a day in your life.* That sounds sweet, and it probably reads well on a pillow or a t-shirt somewhere but it's really a lie. That's because there are millions of people who have passions for which they have no real aptitude. There's a word for that. We call those hobbies.

I believe there is a reason why so many people are hoping that their passion will become their career and perhaps define them. I think it's because we often have false passions. Let's face it, all of us want to be loved. We want to love. We want to be respected. We want to be honored. And this can often drive our passions. When I was a little kid, I thought I wanted to be a doctor. I even read through my mother's medical books and memorized how to do an emergency appendectomy, fantasizing about the day that I'd be on a desert island with someone and they'd grab their gut and I would immediately pull out some sharp instrument and save their life. I could have been such a hero but thank God that never happened. When I got to high school, I started taking biology classes. It was at that point that I realized, neither did I have the passion for medicine or the aptitude to pursue it. Heck, I barely passed biology! What I realized is that what I really wanted was to help people, be respected, make a good living and be loved. That was my real passion. Wanting to be a doctor was a false passion.

What I realized is that what I really wanted was to help people, be respected, make a good living and be loved.

There's an exercise recommended by success author, Dean Graziosi called *The Seven Levels Deep* tool. For example, if you say *I'm passionate about this*, ask, *Why is that important to me?* It really helps to do the exercise with a partner. Write down your answer and then ask, *Why is this important to me?* Write that down and then ask, *Why is that important to me?* Do that four more times as you get deeper to the core of why. At that point, you really start to get to the depth of what your passion is really all about and where it is rooted. It gets past the easy answers and surface stuff. It helps you past the false passions and gets to the core of who you are as a human being and what's really important to you. I've seen people get a little choked-up as their heart is revealed.

The next tip of the triangle in the *Authentic Purpose Compass* is aptitude. When you were a child, did you ever notice that there were kids around you that just seemed to be good at certain things? There was the math kid and the music kid and the athletic kid and the leader kid. Maybe you were one of them. Aptitude alone might feel natural at first and be the thing that friends and family will push you towards. But do you know what you get when you pursue aptitude without passion? Those are called jobs. It's easy to find people working in their aptitude without passion on social media. They are the ones celebrating Fridays and complaining about Mondays. You know what I'm talking about? It's completely understandable to have to live this type of life for a season but this would be miserable if you had to do this for the rest of your life.

The next tip in the *Authentic Purpose Compass* is experience. We talked earlier about Malcolm Gladwell's writing about the 10,000 hours of experience that leads to mastery. Now you might not have 10,000 hours or you may have a lot more, but the experiences and trajectory of your life are critical clues to discovering your authentic purpose. Reflecting back to when you were younger up until now; What skills have you acquired? What jobs have you done? What clubs did you join? What hobbies do you pursue? What network or community have you developed?

> *Your life resume is more than just a list of places that paid you but a tapestry of experiences that have shaped you.*

Now, going through the discovery process is not easy and navigating the trajectory of your life and organization will require strength, stamina and conviction. But imagine the power and joy you could realize by bringing your life and your organization into alignment with your authentic purpose.

Mission

The next of the five elements that form your Mission Manifesto is missions. You might notice that I use the word missions instead of mission. Every day, you see some corporation or organization put up a big plaque stating, *this is our mission*. We're going to do this and this and this. The biggest challenge about that is that sometimes their mission is really kind of a purpose mixed in as a mission. It can become so diluted that it isn't actionable or meaningful or motivating. At best, it makes for a good plaque. After the framers of our constitution stated their purpose, *to form a more perfect union*, they outlined the five missions necessary to fulfill that purpose. These include: *establish justice, insure domestic tranquility, provide for the common defense, promote the general welfare, and secure the blessings of liberty to ourselves and our posterity.*

In his book, *The Jesus Mission*, author Steven K. Scott documents that Jesus actually had 27 missions. When you look at how he approached missions, it looks a lot more like a military mission where maybe you have a purpose, such as *win the war*, but you have multiple missions to complete to fulfill that purpose.

While purpose is a way of life, missions are something where you can actually say, 'Mission accomplished!'

Imagine how much more freeing it is to recognize that you don't have to fit everything onto a notecard. The truth is that most purposes may require three or more missions to fulfill. And over time, you may have to add or delete missions. While purpose is a way of life, missions are something where you can actually say, *Mission accomplished!*

Vision

The third component of your *Mission Manifesto* is vision. Few things are more confusing than the term vision, as it's often confused with purpose, missions, values and goals. When I'm working with our marketing clients, for the sake of clarity, I encourage them to think of it this way; your purpose is your why. Your missions are the things you must accomplish to fulfill your purpose. But your vision is special. Your vision is not just a cluster of words but a picture that is so clear you can see it in vivid detail. If you're like me, when you were a kid, you might have put together puzzles. And what's the first thing you did? You looked at the cover of the box! Once you know what you were working toward, you could sort the pieces, corners here, edges there. And there were times that you mixed up the pieces from different puzzles, kind of like life. The world wants to keep throwing pieces at you and if you don't discern what pieces belong in your puzzle and know where they go, it's easy to be lost and distracted. Ever feel that way? And then there is the frustration of trying to force a puzzle piece from someone else's puzzle that just doesn't belong in your puzzle. All you do is waste time, bend the edges and get frustrated until eventually, you figure out this just doesn't fit.

Your vision is not just a cluster of words but a picture that is so clear you can see it in vivid detail.

What's so powerful is when you discover your vision, you activate a part of the brain that will subconsciously work with you towards its fulfillment. When you get clarity about what you want, what it looks like, it gives so much power to your ability to not only prioritize your activities, but it also comes with emotion. It's that emotion that stirs you to push forward when things get hard.

One of my favorite sayings is, *Hard is good;* though I might never put it on a t-shirt. Hard is good because nothing of significance has ever been done without going through the journey of hard; otherwise we wouldn't call it significant. Otherwise we wouldn't give people medals or trophies if it weren't for the fact that they had to traverse a profound and hard journey to get there. Recognize that you were born for significance.

> *Recognize that you were born for significance.*

Goals

The next element of your *Mission Manifesto* is goals. Goals are important especially as they relate to the 7 Disciplines. It is essential that you get clarity on your goals early because ultimately, you will want to measure progress and you can't measure progress unless you have established some clear goals.

SMARTer Goals

You've most likely seen the acronym, SMART relating to goals. The letters most commonly stand for **specific**, **measurable, achievable, relevant**, and **timely**. I think this is a great tool to help guide goal setting, but I would just change one word, and that would be to change *achievable* to *aspirational*. That's because some of the greatest things (and even the scariest things) that have ever been accomplished in the world didn't look like they were even achievable. For example, in May of 1961, John F. Kennedy said he wanted to land a man on the moon within the decade. Some people thought he was nuts and no one was quite sure how or if it could be done. But by July of 1969, Neil Armstrong landed and walked on the moon.

If you're like me, when you were a little kid, you had all kinds of crazy dreams. But the realistic, and sometimes crushing adult influences brought us back to earth to only think of practical, common sense and achievable goals.

I'm really happy that John F. Kennedy didn't listen when, I'm certain, his critics told him to get his head out of the stars.

You might not see what can truly be achieved if you are stuck thinking that the person you are today is the person responsible for achieving those goals tomorrow.

If you limit yourself to those things that you know you can achieve, you're robbing yourself of perhaps the greatest opportunity to stretch, grow and maybe do something incredible. One of the most powerful things we can learn by stretching is to recognize that aspiration requires personal transformation. You might not see what can truly be achieved if you are stuck thinking that the person you are today is the person responsible for achieving those goals tomorrow. But imagine what could be achieved if they were completed by a growing and transformed you or a growing and transformed team. So, set your sights to shoot beyond achievable and replace the idea of *Achievable* with *Aspirational. It's right to dream even though it might be the scariest and most vulnerable goal you will ever set for yourself.* But imagine what could happen in your life and the lives of others, if we all set more than achievable goals but also focused our energy on dreaming and becoming the person or organization we must become to realize our greatest aspirations.

> *True values are those that manifest in the personality of the organization, usually starting with leadership, and then being expressed through the team.*

Values

The last of the five elements for your *Mission Manifesto* is values. When most organizations list their values, they include words like excellence, integrity, strength, caring, etc. Values might look nice on a plaque, right next to old mission statements, but to be really valuable, they need to be authentic and actionable. I love doing brand personality evaluations with our clients because along with capturing the perceived culture of an organization, what the evaluations really reveal are values. True values are those that manifest in the personality of the organization, usually starting with leadership, and then being expressed through the team. Another thing that makes stated values so important is that it forces an organization to prioritize them through daily decisions. For example, if we talk about goals, things you have to measure are; *How important is winning versus losing? How important is aspiring and doing great things versus being safe? What would happen if absolute excellence threatens margins and sustainability? When does honesty win over caring? Is there a time for discretion over transparency?* These all sound like values judgements. Those are very simple examples, but you get the point. Documenting them won't eliminate difficult discussions, but they will bring clarity as you live in integrity with your brand personality internally and externally through your values.

You'll find again, that this structure is similar to that of the U.S. Constitution. Once, the purpose was established, *...to form a more perfect Union...,* the document outlines the missions necessary to accomplish it, provides clear vision as to how it would be accomplished and then closes with a series of values that, while still debated as to how they should be applied, set guides and boundaries for what we believe. No matter what party is in office, these values, known as the Bill of Rights, still stand as a guiding light to the heart and personality of the United States.

Whether building or reinforcing your organization, launching a new product, brand or campaign, investing in your *Mission Manifesto* will pay dividends in establishing your brand foundation and delivering with conviction and clarity to your team and your markets.

Paradise Point Manifesto

When we were hired to oversee the marketing of a beachfront property in Hawaii, it was essential that we be on the same page with the developer. Honoring this process, the purpose of the engagement was simple; Develop and promote the Paradise Point brand in such a way as to distinguish it from any other beachfront property in Hawaii in order to capture the highest return on investment for the development shareholders. We outlined a variety of missions that we felt were necessary to accomplish this purpose, painted a vision of who might inhabit the estate, set a series of tactical and financial goals, and drafted a set of values in the form of a brand personality that we would express at every possible touchpoint with our markets. The creative process was fun as we crafted the storyline, but no one on the team could imagine the surprise when the launch kicked into gear. Now it's time to meet your markets. One of the challenges I see distracting and diluting an organizational focus is clarity about their markets. In the next chapter, we'll focus on meeting your best markets and how to have a more meaningful and prosperous relationship with them.

Chapter 6

I Only Have Eyes for You

It's easier to love a brand
when the brand loves you back.
Seth Godin

Relationship marketing may seem complex for some, but honestly, it's a lot like falling in love. First you meet someone and decide that there is something special here. Then you decide that you want to have a relationship and the pursuit begins. Presuming that you are not acting like a creeper, you naturally want to know everything about them. You want to know their interests and what pleases them. You find ways to be close to them, to connect and to see if the relationship can blossom into something special. You are thoughtful and proactive. You do this because you really care, and you want every opportunity for this relationship to flourish and be ongoing.

Imagine if we actually treated our markets that way. In a world where we try to systematize and socialize marketing into automated this and managed that, it's no wonder that many client relationships fall off the radar and cause people to feel transactional, uncared for or outright ignored.

Radio DJ

In high school, I had the opportunity to work as the weekend radio DJ at a local college. To get my head in the right frame of mind, one of my mentors shared a story about how radio DJs can frequently lose sight of their market. The reason it can be difficult for DJs to keep their audience in the forefront of their mind is because they simply can't see them. With the advent of the two-person morning drive teams, it got even worse as the hosts would simply banter with each other between segments and their listeners might feel left out or feel that the conversation was not relevant to them. The sales team performed a little intervention and pointed out (using some classic demographic descriptions) that their desirable audience was really, for example, women ages 18-34, or men ages 35-64. But the real brilliance was the addition of an 8x10 frame with a picture of their ideal listener placed between the two DJs. With that, they brought that person into the conversation and before long, instead of a two-way conversation, the DJs were having a three-way conversation. The level of relevance and interest started to pique the interests of that target market once again. Ratings went up and it was immediately recognized that one of the best ways to form a relationship, even if you can't talk to every individual person, was to establish what we call personas, someone that personifies your target audience.

Apple Markets

Personas are a classic way of trying to establish a target market group by trying to segment them in a manner that helps you feel like you know them in a way that you can actually market to them effectively. Take Apple for example. Its classic market segments include teenagers, college students, adults, business people and even young children. Depending upon the product or the industry or the geography, Apple can shape its marketing approach and message in a manner that makes it more relevant to a specific market.

Lady Gaga Markets

Even pop stars like Lady Gaga have market segmentation. While the primary buying market might be people ages 15-30, her management recognizes that she clearly has opportunities for segmentation beyond that core. This led to key partnerships with other artists like Tony Bennett and her highly successful launch into the motion picture world with *A Star is Born*. She also has a very strong connection with the LGBTQ community. When Lady Gaga was growing up and developing her voice in New York City, it was this community that embraced her and invited her to sing at open mics. That relationship created a strong bond that today helps expand her brand message of reaching out to people who feel rejected by family or society and letting them know they are worthy to be loved.

Jesus Markets

As a businessmen and religious leader, Jesus modeled market segmentation. You see this in the relevance of his messaging. For example, he had messaging designed for the religious audience, political figures, the business audience, ethnic minorities, rich, poor, those afflicted with illness, and those who were falsely accused or imprisoned. One of the most important principles that we see modeled is that when it comes to marketing, Jesus' driver wasn't just to engage with people who would buy what he was offering, but instead to actively pursue those he was called to serve. This is a driver that I hope all of us can embrace with sincerity and purpose.

Jesus' driver wasn't just to engage with people who would buy what he was offering, but instead to actively pursue those he was called to serve.

Five Ways to Identify Your Best Markets

I'm often asked, *Who should I be marketing to? Who's my best market?* Each situation is different. But I do have some classic market questions that can help get you started in validating or steering you towards market clarity. The first question regards product relationship. *Who really needs what you are offering?* Then ask, *Which markets offer the highest yield over the life of the relationship?* The next question regards the classic 80/20 rule. *What 20 percent of your market will produce the highest outcomes to fulfill your purpose and missions?*

The Platinum Market Relationship

Where this can really become powerful is with what I call the platinum relationship. Chances are if you've been in business for any season at all, there have been relationships that you have really enjoyed and have been both profitable and meaningful. I call those your platinum clients. These are clients with whom you have shared missions, values and even cultures. These clients are profitable and meaningful because serving them multiplies your missions and purpose. *Which of those clients do you wish you had an additional 10, 100, 1000 or more?*

There is power that happens in the chemistry of a relationship when it's born out of mutual respect, collaboration and connection.

When the Chemistry is Just Right

The last question involves pure relationship. *With what clients do I have a great, mutually beneficial and truly satisfying relationship?* There is a power that happens in the chemistry of a relationship, especially service relationships. When you have them and they are born out of mutual respect, collaboration and connection, these are the relationships that you would like to see flourish and grow. I'd hope that all of your relationships provide this but sometimes business relationships tear you down and exhaust you. At our creative agency, Spirit Media, we've used this guiding question not only to find great clients but also to make us wake up as to when we need to walk away from a client. For example, as a media agency, we believe that we are in a unique position to promote or amplify the message, brand or culture of our clients. When we have discovered that a client (or prospective client) may be promoting hate, deceptive product claims, or have a culture that tears down people, we walk away. The integrity of our agency and the well-being of our team, culture and community are too important to allow anyone to deceive or destroy. Regardless of the criteria you use to choose your best markets, what we know for certain is that the most effective marketers know their audience intimately and the better they know their audience, the more effectively they can make genuine connections and form lasting, meaningful and yes, loving relationships.

The 10 Digit Human Address

Just like the radio DJs, you might not have an opportunity to meet every single one of your markets. But you too can form deeper relationships by developing personas. My friends at NIKE call them muses because they not only serve to inform but to inspire you to form a deeper understanding of them.

Each one of the digits really represent aspects of your persona to help get you closer to them and find where they really live. These digits of the human address are demographics, psychographics, influencers, then the WINOFF formula of wants, interests, needs, objections, fears and frustrations. Finally, we want to understand what their buying journey is.

Demographics

In the case of demographics, we're looking to gather classic information like age, income, gender, occupation, education, their race or ethnicity, where they live and a little bit about their family, like their marital status and family size.

Psychographics

For psychographics, it's great to get a sense of their personality style. At Spirit media we use a personality method called the DISC profile. D stands for dominance, I for influence, S for steadiness and C for compliance. Even though you can't perform a direct DISC profile on your persona, you can look at who your platinum profile might be and then ask the questions about whether they are more dominant, influential, steady or compliant. That will give you a sense of their personality and will help later in determining messaging style and the means you use to communicate.

Influencers

Knowing your markets influencers will also play a critical role as you move forward and start determining the methods you are going to be using to move people along the buying journey. One of the questions that you might ask are, *Who do they value or esteem?* That could include friends or family, coworkers, social influencers, authorities, celebrities, or even brands. Other questions to ask are, *What media do they consume and share? Are they active in social media? And if so, what platforms do they use? Do they watch* television or movies? Broadcast or Netflix? What music do they listen to? What brands do they drive or wear? Are they book readers or book consumers through Kindle or audible? Do they like to read certain publications? And how active are they on the web and do they read blogs?

WINOFF Formula

Let's talk about the WINOFF formula. I call it the WINOFF formula thanks to a brilliant consultant, Eugene Wallace, who pointed out that the six drivers I use to capture the mindset of my persona actually forms a clever acronym.

Wants

The first is W, and that stands for **wants**. Knowing the wants of your persona is very important but recognize their wants don't always drive the decision. They frequently consist of things like *one day it'd be nice if*, or *someday we ought to...* It doesn't make a want less important than a need but wants usually are prioritized below needs as secondary objectives and they usually will not drive a sale because they lack urgency.

Interests

Next is **interests**. Understanding the interests of the client will allow you to dig deeper in the possibility of forming relationships. Finding shared missions, shared hobbies and bridges will allow you to build a gateway into a relationship.

Needs

Next is **needs**. Needs are critical because needs have urgency. Needs are not only what your market feels is absolutely necessary but there is usually a clear deadline to when they need that need fulfilled. Dr. Angela Lauria from the Author Incubator asks a brilliant question to help authors understand the needs of their prospective readers. Her question is, *What will make your readers dream come true?* This is a great question because it also attaches deep emotion which is necessary to move people, especially in a complex sale.

Objections

O stands for **objections**. Objections are the spoken or unspoken concerns that you will need to address usually because they perceive that you can't satisfy their wants or their needs or their fears or frustrations. Understanding objections are great in that they can reveal things that are not obvious on the surface but must be addressed.

Fears

F is for **fears**. Fears are one of the things that haunts your potential client and one of the greatest fears is failure. Failure means not addressing their needs. Failure means that you missed a mission critical deadline. Fears mean that you won't get it done on time or that there will be cost overruns. Knowing them is critical so that you can address them upfront.

Frustrations

The last F in the WINOFF formula is **frustrations**. Let's face it, even if you could address people's fears, frustrations are born out of not addressing their wants or needs. *Do they need peace of mind? Do they need more effective communication? Do they need it more frequently? Do you need to make them look good in front of their boss or their donor or their co-workers?* If you don't address these things that are very frustrating, know that this frustration will play back in a script over and over in their head as they decide whether to not only buy from you now but whether they want to engage with you later. Also note that the peace of mind you give them will be the launchpad for them becoming your ambassador later.

The great beauty of the WINOFF formula is discovering the key message and emotional drivers that will help us craft relevant messaging.

The great beauty of the WINOFF formula is discovering the key message and emotional drivers that will help us craft relevant messaging. Knowing their wants, interests, needs, objections, fears and frustrations is a critical ingredient in crafting great messaging and it's a very enlightening part of our client workshops and coaching sessions.

Buying Journey

When it comes to buying journey there really is a classic model for the journey that follows these steps. Step one is awareness. Step two is learning. Step three is understanding. Step four is embracing. Step five is buy-in. Step six is action. Each one of these steps is important and require that you not only manage but you help facilitate this journey. Are there points along the journey where there may be obstacles? Are there areas that cause them to pause? Do we seem to lose them at a consistent point? Understanding the buying journey is not only an essential insight into your markets but it will play a vital role in prioritizing the resources and methods necessary in your sales and marketing process.

Knowing these fundamental aspects of your persona will directly relate to the success of your relationship with them because your relationship will be directly correlated to your capacity to identify and satisfy your buyer's emotional and intellectual needs.

Application - Paradise Point Persona

Let me bring you up to date on our Paradise Point persona. After doing extensive research about people who would buy high-end properties in Hawaii, it was clear that we had a subject that represented the perfect persona and the one that represented the highest likelihood of purchase. It turned out that the demographic was a white male, age 45 to 65 and living in the United States. From a psychographic standpoint. Their mindset was, *I've earned this. I've worked hard for this.*

From a wants standpoint they hoped to be able to share this property with others. They wanted to be able to showcase it in a way that established that they had earned it. When it comes to needs; they wanted a celebrity level quality and feel. It was important that this wasn't just a home but really a trophy. As to their fears, most of them felt that they could not live up to their own standards and that this home really was an expression of what they had aspired to be. When it came to frustrations, the home did have limited availability and it was expensive. There's not an unlimited supply of beachfront properties on Hawaii and it made finding just the perfect property a very elaborate task.

One of our objections surprised us because we had not developed property in Hawaii before. We were shocked to hear that Oahu actually comes with a little bit of a stigma. People like Oprah Winfrey and Bill Gates are living on the less inhabited islands like Kauai. Oahu was considered the pedestrian island. As a result, we had to work hard to position the Oahu beachfront property as having as much esteem as any of the other islands. World-class medical facilities conveniently located near the property also helped attract this age group.

The buying journey was actually pretty easy when you're purchasing properties in the 5, 10, 15, 20-million-dollar range. You still go through a real estate agent. Real estate agents are very much about word-of-mouth and they listen to the winds of perceived markets and trends so there'd be ways that we could leverage language and create experiences to be able to connect with them and make sure that our property, the Paradise Point property, was top of mind among real estate agents.

Coincidentally, the biggest influencers were first, their peers, other real estate agents. Second were island power influencers and third was media. The people that we believed were most likely to buy the Paradise Point home esteemed successful people and esteemed celebrities.

These were people that they were, or aspired to be, so we wanted to make sure that we were connected in some way to them to elevate their perception of this property.

How to Research Your Persona

I frequently get asked what ways we can use to gather this information to make sure that we are actually creating the correct persona. Well, there's some classic ways to do that. The first is good old fashion market research. You can do this on the web, or you can hire companies that do market research. In either case, market research provides some general demographics that can help frame markets or potential markets for your product or service.

Another way of researching is with focus groups. Over the years, depending upon the nature of the project, we have conducted numerous focus groups, either by phone, online or in person. Focus groups are great in that it gives you a chance to not only ask questions but to follow up on that question and really dig in to make sure that you are hearing what really drives their buying decisions. You can also do surveys yourself or hire a company to conduct surveys for your target audience.

Another resource is interviews. If you have those platinum clients, they are a gold mine to be able to go back and ask if you can get a little bit more information about how they found you, why they chose you, why they continue to work with you, and a number of other questions that will help form and shape a potential persona where you can duplicate that platinum customer as many times as you like.

But nearly as reliable as most of these is what I call institutional knowledge. Institutional knowledge is the knowledge that you and your team already have about your markets. Chances are you've met them. You know them and you know a lot about them.

Most institutional knowledge is 80 to 90 percent correct and will get you well on your way to helping develop a reliable persona. The beauty of using some of these other methodologies is that it's not unusual to have 5 to 10 percent of some surprises that emerge when you dig a little deeper. Knowing these extra bits of information can mean the difference between hitting the target and hitting the bullseye.

Don't just look for people who will buy from you but look for those whom you are called to serve.

Relationships Take Work, but God Knows

The idea of knowing your markets and then effectively reaching them sometimes can be the scariest part of growing your organization. The good news is rooted in the lesson we learned earlier in this chapter. Don't just look for people who will buy from you but look for those whom you are called to serve. Jesus said that every hair on our heads is numbered and he said that to emphasize how important you are to him. Now that's intimate knowledge! What that also means is that he knows your markets intimately as well. Our job is to follow that calling to serve, and then trust and honor the process by loving your clients and forming rich, loving and meaningful relationships.

Now that we know more about our markets, the natural question is, *What do I say?* In the next chapter, you are going to learn the most reliable recipe for crafting the perfect message every time.

Chapter 7

Whispering Sweet Nothings

*The greatest challenge of communication
is the illusion that it is taking place.*

George Bernard Shaw

When I was dating my high school sweetheart who would eventually become my wife, I would occasionally lean over in the car or maybe at the movie theater to whisper something special to her. You know what I mean, that special something that you think is sweet that will elicit some type of cute reaction. To my frustration, I rarely did get the reaction I was looking for. This actually happened for months until one day she revealed to me that as a child she had an injury to her inner ear and was virtually deaf on one side. It struck me that despite my best intentions, I truly was just whispering nothings. This wasn't just an awkward way to start a relationship, it's a vivid example of what happens when we aren't effectively applying the discipline of message.

Meet Your Reticular Activating System

This challenge happens every day in the marketplace, not because people are shutting us down from a physiological handicap but because of sheer volume. Some marketing researchers estimate that we receive somewhere in the neighborhood of five to ten thousand brand messages a day. It's no wonder that we shut some of them down. In fact, we have this fabulous system called the reticular activating system in our brain that filters out repetitive and nonessential information. Think about it. You receive thousands of data points of information every day through sight, hearing, smelling, tasting and touch. Even right now, the texture of your clothing is touching your skin and sending signals to your brain. But are you conscious of it? Most likely not. That's because the reticular activating system is working for you to filter out those messages that really aren't relevant. Did you ever buy a car and then suddenly notice that it seems like there are a lot more of that model on the road? That's your reticular activating system at work. When you purchased your car, you were very conscious of the make and model and, in the buying process, this car became relevant to you. That's why you see them all of a sudden. It's not that hundreds of other people decided to buy one the same day you did. Instead, the make and model of car became relevant to you and now you see it like you never did before.

Millennials shift attention so rapidly, in part, because they have a highly developed BS filter.

What About Millennials?

Millennials get a bad reputation because people accuse them of having a short attention span. The real truth is that millennials do consume data, especially screen data, at a very high rate, but that rate at which they switch screens is not really driven by an attention span issue. Millennials shift attention so rapidly, in part, because they have a highly developed BS filter. The fact that they are bombarded with more brand messages than any generation in the history of mankind has allowed them to develop a more efficient system for determining whether content is relevant or not relevant. I think we can all agree that the vast majority of marketing messages today aren't very relevant. That's where smart marketing and messaging becomes so critical.

Message Principles and Best Practices

Jesus didn't have to compete with thousands of brand messages, but he did live in a world filled with oppression, disease, hatred and poverty, just to name a few. Like any communicator, it was essential that he communicate in a highly relevant way that captured the attention of the people in a meaningful and memorable way. Jesus was known for his parables and when you look at the majority of his parables, they relate to things that not only were relevant then but are relevant today such as farming, fishing, family and culture. But the majority of them were framed around the areas of business and leadership and at the heart of them, how to really understand God and conduct all relationships lovingly and honorably. Jesus set the bar for effective messaging and modeled some principles that were not only practiced by some of the great philosophers but are practiced today by some of the most influential leaders of our time.

- The first principle is that the message must honor and operate in harmony with your purpose and missions.
- The next principle is that the message must honor the market to whom you are speaking with real relevance.
- The message must be authentic and sincere.
- The message must be compelling and transferable.

Jesus was such a great communicator that we see him leveraging some of the most powerful and timeless practices within the context of his teaching. For example, we see him repeating concepts to shape themes and also using parables to support understanding and retention. In my early television advertising days, I learned the seven-touch rule. In short, it was the belief that you needed to touch your market a minimum of seven times before they would actually hear and retain the message. It still is a common practice in branding. When you think of it, it's kind of like a dripping water torture or like a tattoo. The term tattoo actually comes from the Polynesian islands where they would dip a piece of sharpened wood in ink and they would tap it into the skin. The continual tapping, tat tat tat tat tat would press the ink under the skin and that tapping became the term tattoo.

> *Most people are becoming more resistant to sales pitches unless they are softer or accompanied by story, shock, humor or extreme value and relevance.*

Repetition is a very effective way for a market to retain a message. Though, like nagging, we are finding that most people are becoming more resistant to sales pitches unless they are softer or accompanied by story, shock, humor or extreme value and relevance. I say compelling because it's the only way that your message will be truly remembered and shared. Compelling makes it transferable because people will want to talk about you, their experience with you and the incredible work that you're doing.

PTSD vs PTG

Another practice that we see in Jesus work was the power of profound experiences and messages together. In other words, when someone has a profound experience, physiological or psychological, the greater the likelihood of retention. Unlike the subtlety of a tattoo-like model, profound experiences have the power to make instant and lasting brand impressions. Soldiers who have traveled overseas and had to face real life battle situations face the risk of experiencing post-traumatic stress disorder (PTSD). This is the consequence of having experienced something so profound that it burns a brand impression on the brain.

Profound experiences have the power to make instant and lasting brand impressions.

An area that is less known is the research in the area of post-traumatic growth. Post-traumatic growth (PTG) is positive psychological change as a result of adversity. A dear friend of mine, and author of the book, *I'm No Hero*, Captain Charlie Plumb, was captured and imprisoned in Vietnam for six years. He like many of the soldiers, including Senator John McCain, experienced traumatic circumstances but something powerful happened. Thanks to neuroplasticity, the brain's ability to change, allowed these officers, who despite having experienced traumatic circumstances, actually displayed positive outcomes from the tragedy. Imagine how powerful the outcome could be if you were to introduce an incredibly positive experience in a profound or experiential way. Imagine the power of the branding impression when you literally sear a positive chemical impression on the minds of your market associated with you and your brand. Jesus was a master of this practice.

The Perfect Message Recipe

Now it's time for the message recipe. In the last chapter we talked about the WINOFF formula from your target markets wants, interests, needs, objections, fears and frustrations. When you craft a message, it's important that you speak to these areas of interest directly. Many marketers make the great mistake of telling their sales story by shoving it down people's throats. Most people are not primarily interested in your story, but instead hearing how you can connect with their story. And of course, they don't want to be sold. They're listening for the things that are relevant to them.

Remember the reticular activating system? They are listening and will perk up when you address those elements that are relevant to them. That means that if you speak in a relevant manner, you will trigger the reticular activating system and it will open the filters so that you can be heard. If you do not speak in a manner that's relevant to them, they may give you the courteous nod from time to time, but your words sound more like the squawking teacher in a *Charlie Brown* episode. For this reason, your message is going to be a strategic combination to align with the WINOFF formula.

Now that you have the key messages that your market wants to hear, you must align it with the key messages that you believe your market must hear to understand what you can do for them that will guide them to a mutually beneficial relationship. The ingredients for this part of the message consists of features, benefits, benefits of the benefits, proof, your differentiators, or unique selling proposition, and cost - FBBPDC. I know, it's not as cool of an acronym but you get the point.

---

*The features validate the offering, but it
is the benefits that really
create excitement.*

Features and Benefits

Let's start with features. Much like the window sticker
on the outside of a new car, your market does need to
know what you offer. This is important but how many
times did you read the window sticker and scream, O*h boy,
this one's for me!* Of course not. The features validate the
offering, but it is the benefits that really create excitement.
After all, it's the benefits that really get at the reason why
we are really buying the car and guess what? Most of the
reasons are driven by emotion.

Benefits of the Benefits

There's an old advertising story about the days when
automatic door locks were launched as a luxury feature on
cars. The feature itself was not a hot seller and few were
coming to dealerships asking for it. But one day, the
marketers got a hold of the idea and began marketing it as
a *peace of mind* benefit. *Imagine the peace of mind of knowing that
while your family is traveling down the road, your children aren't*

going to accidentally open the door and tumble out onto the pavement. That may sound a little gruesome, but it worked. Automatic door locks are not just for the luxury set but are common on most car models today. That's the power of benefits.

Do know that all benefits are not as instantly connected in the minds of your markets, so it is smart to add to your message, the benefits of the benefit. In our car example, we could have added that your child won't have to go to the hospital or be injured for life or hate you because you didn't protect them. Parents have a gift for going deep on the benefits of the benefits, especially as it relates to fear. You, on the other hand, may have to spell out your benefits of the benefit more strategically with your product or service.

Proof must be woven in as a centerpiece of your marketing message as it relates to the benefit of your product.

Prove it!

Next is proof. It's common for marketers to talk about their product and tell people how great it is. Just know that every person that is receiving that message already has a secret shield up that is saying, *I'm holding you at arm's length because I think you want to sell me,* or *I think that you are more interested in getting money out of me than solving my problem.* The best way to address this form of objection is to provide proof. Proof can come in many forms. For example, you could provide facts, statistics, case studies, testimonials or stories. In any case, proof must be woven in as a centerpiece of your marketing message as it relates to the benefit of your product.

Woven into your message must be your unique selling proposition and differentiation.

What Makes You Different?

The next ingredient is your unique selling proposition or differentiation. Let's face it, you're not the only one out there offering what you're offering. You have competition and if your prospective clients are smart, they're doing a little homework as to who can solve their problems, deliver at the right time and deliver at the right price. That's why woven into your message must be your unique selling proposition and differentiation. Tragically, most organizations are weak on differentiation because it usually takes a lot of work and they have no real objectivity about their organization. I get a chuckle out of those who want to wave the years of service as their primary differentiation. Let's be honest. You may have been in business for a thousand years, but it doesn't mean you have meaningful differentiation to make your product worthy to buy over someone else. Consider using the journalism method just as a means of self-exploration. Ask yourself:

- Does who we are make us unique or different?
- Does what we do make us unique or different?
- Does why we do what we do make us unique or different?
- Does where we do what we do make us unique or different?
- Does when we do what we do (like on time) make us unique or different??

- Does how we do what we do make us unique or different?

Compare the answers to these questions and look at other things that are important and relevant to your customer from the WINOFF information to create that really unique differentiation. The WINOFF review will not only help you craft a story of differentiation but will make sure it is uniquely relevant to your market.

Pleasure and Pain

The last ingredient is cost. When I say cost, most people are thinking about the cost of your product or service. What I'm saying is, W*hat's the cost of not buying from you?* At the core of our decision-making process is the contrast between pleasure and pain.

What's the cost of not buying from you?

The pleasure side of all of us makes us want to aspire to achieve some outcome. However, the pain side is usually driven around the emotional side of fear. Your markets might not talk upfront about their fears but know that, in most cases, it is the greater driver. A lot of people are afraid to be open about the cost of not doing business with them. You can be blunt or imply it, but if you don't weave the cost of not doing business with you within the tapestry of your message, you would be failing to tell the whole story and your message would be incomplete.

If you have trouble determining what the cost of not doing business with you really is, you might have a product problem so go back and work with your team and make sure that you can make a very strong case.

Finding Your Core Message

Depending on your product or service, you may have one to as many as five or more personas who reflect different audiences for your products and services. In which case, going through this exercise will develop what we typically call themes and threads also referred to as a core messages versus unique messages. Once you've gone through this exercise, I recommend displaying each one of your personas and aligning all their wants, interest, needs, objections, fears, and frustrations - WINOFFs. You'll find that they share a lot of them, but some are unique.

Then on the **FBBPDC** side, identify your features, benefits, benefits of the benefits, proof points, differentiators and cost that you can directly associate as satisfying your prospect **WINOFF**. It's this glorious intersection that frames your core messages. These are the things that are central to you and universal to virtually every one of your personas.

Unique Messages

Just as you did when you were aligning the persona **WINOFF** and your **FBBPDC** to discover your core message, you will find needs that are unique to an individual persona. Whether it is their particular needs or if it relates to the product they want to buy from you, this demands that we craft unique messages. As you survey your personas, look for those needs that are not addressed by your core message and then isolate them for this unique persona. Once again, look at how your **FBBPDC** can satisfy that unique message and now you have customized it for them. When you honor the Perfect

Message Recipe, like a beautiful tapestry, the vivid colors of your brand message and the nuances that are unique to the different personas can shine with new clarity and strength.

When you honor the Perfect Message
Recipe, like a beautiful tapestry,
the vivid colors of your brand message
and the nuances that are unique to the
different personas can shine with
new clarity and strength.

Paradise Point Messaging

Let's revisit our Paradise Point case study and how getting the messaging right was critical to our success. If you remember our primary persona, they were looking for something very special because they were very special. We produced a lot of resources but at the heart was the message. While virtually every brand becomes stronger when it is attached to a story, our team agreed that it was essential that this message would be best delivered in the form of a story.

Some of the actual language read as follows: *Kailua is the strength of the earth, the power of the winds and the magic of the sky and heavens, a territory once treasured by kings, a possession prized and protected by a benevolent family. Paradise Point is a rare jewel, a sparkling gem that has been hidden from view for more than a century and now the Paradise Point estate is your rare opportunity to own a prized piece of heaven. Nestled between the Pacific Ocean and a private canal, the estate's premiere location and celebrity level security conveys a bold statement of exclusivity. Paradise Point estates brings harmony between sea land and sky. It's a lifestyle nothing less than perfect.*

Note how the initial language was short on features but deep on emotional benefits. We emphasized key terms that were attached to the wants and needs of our persona such as rare opportunity, exclusivity, celebrity, unique. They were subtle, but they were at the core of getting to the emotional connection that someone was going to believe and decide to investigate and hopefully purchase.

Words have power and we have the power to make a profound difference in this world with the words we choose to use.

Your Message Has the Power to Change Lives

Over the life of my career, I've had the opportunity to direct live events, television programs and webcasts around the world to millions. However, there was a point when I was directing a show that really hit me. As I was listening to the speaker, I found myself stirred by the fact that their language was mean spirited, hateful and he demonized people just for believing differently than he did. That felt so wrong in my heart and it wasn't like anything that I saw Jesus model, except for the strong language he used when he was talking about religious hypocrites. I had to consider the role I was playing in advancing this message. Even though it wasn't coming out of my mouth, I was advancing his message, elevating his message and making it possible for others to be subject to his hatred. I made a decision that I would never do that again.

Doesn't it make sense for all of us who are leaders and communicators to make sure that the things that come out of our mouths are bringing health and healing?

It was after this, that I came across a letter from one of Jesus' followers, Paul of Tarsus. In the letter, he's encouraging people to have a healthy mindset by being proactive about what we allow our heads and hearts to think about. Then it really hit me. If this is the prescription for what healthy thinking is about, doesn't it make sense for all of us who are leaders and communicators to make sure that the things that come out of our mouths are bringing health and healing? As to the things we should be thinking about, Paul listed things that are *authentic*, things that *respectable and honorable*, things that are worthy of *merit*, things that awaken *awe and wow*, things that are *beautiful and appealing*, things that are *admirable and excellent*, things that are *commendable*. What I want to emphasize is that words have power and we have the power to make a profound difference in this world with the words we choose to use.

What we just covered can be pretty complex and difficult if you are doing it alone or even with a self-guided small group. So, as a special gift, I made a video that walks you through the ultimate message recipe. This is a great teaching and will help add understanding as you work to develop or refine your perfect message. Watch it by yourself or with your team and walk through the exercise. It will help if you do it, at least, with one other person to hold yourself accountable and make sure you really honor the process. It's also a preview of an online workshop coming soon that your entire team can study and apply. This video gift is absolutely free, and you will find it along with another video gift at www.7DRM.com/eastereggs.

Now that you have the recipe for making the perfect message, it's time to learn how to amplify the impact of that message. That strategy and the way to truly multiply the reach of your message is what we will discuss in the next chapter.

Chapter 8

Decisions Aren't
Made in a Vacuum

*There are exceptional people out there
who are capable of starting epidemics.
All you have to do is find them.*

Malcolm Gladwell

Around the time that Jesus was about 30 years old, he, his disciples and his mother were invited to one of the most famous weddings in history, the wedding at Cana. At this time, it was likely that Jesus was not only a respected teacher and rabbi, but also the esteemed heir to his father's business. Whether the wedding was a humble affair or if it attracted some major dignitaries, there is no question that it was a large gathering, probably exceeding a thousand people. As was the tradition, the wedding feast would last probably five to seven days.

As the story unfolds, sometime during the wedding feast, they ran out of wine. When Jesus was notified by his mother, he agreed to have the servants fill ceremonial jars with about 120-180 gallons of water so that he could transform them into what was reported to be some very fine wine. Jesus was about to leverage the discipline of messengers.

Greatest Product Launch in History?

While theologians and historians alike will debate the location and the exact timing of the wedding, the fact that it continues to this day to be such an iconic event is masterful. At the risk of being sacrilegious, I would consider it to be the greatest product launch in history. Remember in the last chapter when we talked about how profound experiences can create an instantaneous brand? This was Jesus' first recorded public miracle and it's very likely that this event fueled a viral phenomenon about Jesus. Just consider the multiple references to strangers approaching him later in hopes of experiencing his miracle power.

Greatest Merger in History?

Jesus' success at establishing a movement was, in large part, because he was the master of acquiring and leveraging messengers. Shortly before the wedding feast, one of his early and most impactful messenger acquisitions was his relationship with John the Baptist. In a single afternoon, Jesus essentially acquired all of John's followers, estimated to range from a minimum of 3,000 to 5,000 people. Again, at the risk of sounding sacrilegious, I would classify this as one of the greatest mergers or at least, joint ventures, in history. My point is, both the wedding and the merger with John the Baptist were strategic ingredients early in Jesus' public ministry as a vehicle to create compelling, viral experiences while building an army of ambassadors.

A great message, when spoken through the right mouth will be powerfully amplified and multiplied.

The Multiplying Power of Ambassadors

Whether we call them influencers, affluencers, advocates, champions, endorsers, ambassadors, multipliers or messengers, this core concept holds true. A great message, when spoken through the right mouth will be powerfully amplified and multiplied. This is the real model and complete power behind word-of-mouth marketing. It not only shares the message, it multiplies the impact of the message.

Of course, Jesus didn't stop there. He continued to connect with young and old, rich and poor, prisoners and free, servants and leaders. This was central to his work. He created ambassadors with his followers and inner circle. Later, he would advance his message all over the known world with ambassadors who had influence to reach unique cultures and geographies. Perhaps the most important lesson we can capture here is that Jesus wasn't just looking for followers; he was strategically looking to build an ongoing ambassador network. The same holds true for you. Your goal should not be to just find clients, but to leverage ambassadors who can multiply your message and impact.

Your goal should not be to just find clients, but to leverage ambassadors who can multiply your message and impact.

The Ambassador Model Today

We see this model practiced today by some of the most successful companies in the world including Zappos, Amazon, Google, Facebook and Apple. Consider Apple for example. They were able to survive and thrive in a tough competitive market thanks to near-religious brand ambassadorship of their Mac Evangelists. Their connection with the creative community was brilliant as this group was both vocal and had the unique advantage of being media influencers. Zappos broke new ground in online footwear with exceptional service that compelled customers to share their experiences and become ambassadors. Google and especially Facebook built easily transferrable services by creating platforms that urged and compelled people to share. Amazon became the online giant in large part because they became the easiest and most accessible ambassador for millions of products and services. Yes, becoming an ambassador for others can be a central piece of a business model. Ever heard of affiliate marketing?

Common Ambassador Types

Brand ambassadors can take many forms. For example, there are the authority/ambassadors such as sports stars, celebrities, musicians and thought leaders. They are essentially ambassadors for their own brand and their influence rises with the success of their career.

Then there are celebrity/ambassadors where the same celebrities can be ambassadors for another brand, essentially attaching their brand value to another brand. We especially see this relationship between athletic companies and athletes. The athletic company simply expands the depth and reach of their brand by attaching an athlete brand thereby using this celebrity as the embodiment of the brand. This is powerful when you have the right relationship. Every time they hit the field or court, the athletic company brand is reinforced and multiplied.

There are spokespeople/ambassadors that may not embody the brand, but their celebrity attaches relationship, esteem and possibly trust. People like

William Shatner, Jerry Seinfeld, Tina Fey or Matthew McConaughey are common examples.

Some companies go so far as to create a character/ambassador. It is the hope that by developing brand characters, it will cause you to like their brand in a way that no human ambassador could pull-off. This is sensitive territory as some characters like those from the GEICO campaigns or my childhood favorite, Tony the Tiger, may play well with audiences. Other characters, like the Taco Bell chihuahua, which I keep in my office, were ultimate failures in part, because it sent a questionable message about what type of meat was really in the tacos. A little more market homework would have revealed that early.

Keys to Great Ambassadors

Over the years, our creative agency, Spirit Media has worked with a number of celebrities and esteemed authorities as brand ambassadors for our clients. Regardless of what types of ambassadors you choose for your strategy, there are some consistent guidelines that I would encourage you to consider:

1. The ability to repeat a brand message.

2. The ability to articulate relevant aspects of your brand message.

3. The ability to expand the geographic reach of your brand.

4. The ability to expand a brand audience.

5. The ability to amplify a brand message.

6. The ability to move your prospective client more efficiently along the buyer journey.

7. They embody the brand in key personality qualities.

8. They contain the character qualities that you want associated with your brand.

9. They validate the brand through esteemed association.

10. They validate the brand through enthusiastic and sincere endorsement.

Super Ambassadors

Some of these brand ambassadors are so powerful in that while they are extremely successful in their own careers, their personal brand stock is so high that companies covet the opportunity to attach themselves to these super-ambassadors. Harvard University, for example lists Lady Gaga as one of the highest paid brand ambassadors in the world. Other brand ambassadors can be other non-competing brands, such as the symbiotic brand relationship between motion picture companies and fast food establishments. They multiply their reach to a shared audience by leveraging each other's brand influence.

---

*A great brand ambassador
will embody your brand,
will multiply your brand intellectually,
emotionally, and spiritually.*

While no ambassador is perfect, the hope is that a great brand ambassador will embody your brand, will multiply your brand intellectually, emotionally, and spiritually in that they radiate the spirit and the essence of your brand. This will be especially important as we move into methods in the next chapter. We want to make sure that every touchpoint within your organization, whether it be an ambassador or marketing tactic, builds your brand. If you don't pay attention, they could just as easily undermine your brand.

Who Could be Your Best Ambassador?

In a perfect world, some of your best ambassadors are your clients. These are the people who have relationships with other people who could be your new clients and when it comes to trust, these are the most trusted ambassadors to people they know. Your client/ambassadors are living proof points to the quality of your product or service when they speak on your behalf. They are like gold and there is a program that I would recommend that you consider implementing to make sure that you maintain healthy ambassador relationships.

Establishing an ARM Program

You've heard the term, customer relationship management or CRM for short. Those systems typically take a prospect through the buying journey all the way through the sale and then, hopefully renewal. The challenge is that the success of the system is usually attached to the transaction. Client engagement, for the purpose of referrals, is usually casual and non-systematic at best. However, if you're trying to multiply your reach, establish an ambassador relationship management program, or ARM for short. While we hope that every client becomes a raving ambassador, a formal ARM program is reserved for the strategic ones who reflect the qualities of a great ambassador. These are extremely important people, so it should be highly personalized. It doesn't mean that you have to meet with everybody face-to-face, but it should be tiered as to how much you engage them based on their wishes and their value to the program. Also consider that while they serve your marketing interests, your best relationships will grow deeper as you seek to serve them in those ways that advance their missions and help them fulfill their purposes and goals.

The Paradise Point Ambassador Strategy

Ambassadors played a critical role with the Paradise Point project because so much of the buying journey involved a close-knit community of real estate agents. We assembled a multilayered campaign by first identifying who the most influential real estate agents were on the islands. Second, we researched who they esteemed, outside of other agents, and who could influence them. In this particular case, we found that local business leaders, political leaders, and esteemed nonprofit organizations could elevate the value of association with our property. Third, we looked at public relations and the press as ambassadors as a vehicle for creating a climate that would build anticipation and would compel people to notice and talk. While there were other high-end beachfront properties on the island, there were few properties that were talked about in the press and we wanted to make Paradise Point special. We engaged PR/ambassador services in Europe, Asia and throughout the United States targeting key publications that we knew would not only elevate the esteem of the property but would get in the minds of our island influencers. Of course, it didn't hurt to start seeding possible awareness for our potential buyers. A lesson that emerged later was the recognition that you never stop building your ambassador network. This should be obvious from the life of Jesus. If you are building your ambassador network well, you'll find that ambassadors attract other ambassadors and the machine goes to work for you. We definitely saw that happen in a very big way as the Paradise Point campaign grew.

If you are building your ambassador network well, you'll find that ambassadors attract other ambassadors and the machine goes to work for you.

The Danger of Ignoring Ambassadors

Jesus had less than four years to build an army of ambassadors that could make a profound impact that would change the world. If you're like most organizations, you want results now and the temptation is to skip some of these disciplines and jump to marketing tactics. I beg you not to do that. It not only results in falling into the trap of just mimicking other tactics and methods, but it robs you of the synergy that makes the 7DRM Strategy so powerful. If it seems hard, I would agree that it takes time and work to do it right. But would you rather copy and hope or leverage the greatest marketing model in history? That's also one of the reasons that we are here for you and offer workshops and coaching to help you navigate the journey that is right for you. This chapter talked about how your message can be amplified through ambassadors. In the next chapter, we're going to talk about the principles that will help guide you to choosing the very best methods and tactics to not only empower your ambassadors but accelerate the buying journey for your clients.

Chapter 9

Chocolates & Flowers

Good tactics can save even the worst strategy.
Bad tactics will destroy even the best strategy.

George Patton

After I had my death experience, I needed to reconsider everything in my life and one of the things that I had to revisit was the concept of love. I think the Greeks got it right when they explained that there are many forms of love and not every form is romantic. I realized more than ever, that along with greater love and appreciation for my life, I also felt greater love for others. As a result, if you know me, chances are very good that I've told you that I love you. When the time comes that I will actually face my last day alive on earth, I not only want to depart knowing that I expressed love but, perhaps more important, that you know you are loved. This gets even more exciting when you consider that one of the greatest opportunities we have as leaders is to leverage our organization as an instrument of love. Every day, we get to love our venders, our employees and we get to love our clients.

---

*Do unto others as they
would wish done unto them.*

The Platinum Rule

In a romantic relationship, people might try to court each other by showering them with gifts like chocolates and flowers. In a business setting, one of the greatest gifts you can shower on your clients comes from the platinum rule. Most people know the golden rule; *Do unto others as you would wish done unto you.* The platinum rule says, *Do unto others as they would wish done unto them.* When you put that rule into practice inside your entire organization, what that means is our work becomes an act of love. By serving each other, including our clients in a manner that honors them and their buying journey, we are free to look at tactics and methods in a whole new light. We are no longer bound to mimic tactics and methods that everybody says we have to use, but instead, can focus on those tactics that honor our missions and the audiences we are called to serve.

Tactics versus Strategy

I use the word, *tactics* a lot and before we go much further, let's get some clarity on what I mean. Tactics come from a Greek root *(taktikós)* which means to order or arrange, just as you would if you were arranging foot soldiers for battle. This is different from strategy, which comes from the Greek root *(stratēgía)* meaning military general. In a military setting, Dictionary.com explains the difference this way: *Strategy is the utilization, during both peace and war, of all of a nation's forces, through large-scale, long-range planning and development, to ensure security or victory. Tactics deals with the use and deployment of troops in actual combat.* In other words, your strategy should lead and drive your organizational and campaign driven plans, not your tactics. Your tactics, on the other hand, serve to fulfill the objectives of your strategy. Have you ever heard the term, *the tail wagging the dog?* That's what happens when your marketing meetings place tactics before strategy. They are easy to identify. Those are the meetings that are led with _what_ we want to do versus _why_ we want to do. I've been in a lot of those meetings and while they can be creative and fun, they are mostly a waste of time and money for lack of a strategic foundation. That's also why this chapter is so deep in the book. We needed to establish a strategic foundation with the other disciplines.

Strategic Questions Regarding Tactics

At this point, it would be wise to review your organizational or campaign purpose, missions, vision, goals and values. Keep them in front of you as not to lose sight of them. Just for the sake of example, I work with a lot of organizations who need to improve on the *Marketing Big Three* (as I like to call them) of brand management, sales enablement and lead generation. Now, as you consider the methods that you may need to implement to fulfill these marketing needs, here are some strategic questions to consider:

- Will your methods honor your brand?
- Will your methods honor the purpose and mission of your organization, and the campaign in which they'll be used?
- Will your methods honor your market with relevance and value?
- Will your methods honor your markets' buying journey?

- Will your methods honor your markets' media consumption behavior?
- Will your methods amplify and clarify your messages?
- Will your methods empower and enable your messengers?
- Will your methods be measurable?
- Will your methods operate in harmony such that they multiply the impact of your brand?
- Can I afford these methods?
- Do I have the expertise to manage these methods?
- Do I have the capacity to develop and manage these methods?
- Do I have the objectivity to see my organization and this campaign clearly?

I want to emphasize that this chapter is not designed to tell you exactly what to do for your organization. That is a personal decision based upon some of the strategic criteria we just discussed. However, for the value of reviewing some tactics, I think it's smart to think of these two categories. This is hardly a comprehensive list but consider that these two categories are not only different but require different levels of expertise to execute well. The first group is offline tactics. They include:

- TV
- Radio
- Print
- Billboards
- Signage
- Public speaking
- Networking
- Direct mail
- Public relations
- Events

The online world includes:

- Web sites
- Search Engine Optimization (SEO)
- Pay Per Click (PPC)
- Analytics
- Data mining
- Social media
- Blogs
- Vlogs
- Content marketing

- Video production
- Product placement
- Email
- Podcasts
- Webcasts
- App development

What Tactics Did Jesus Use?

When we start talking about actual tactics, especially as it relates to Jesus as marketer, a common question I get is (and it's usually said a little sarcastically), *What tactics did Jesus use?* Let's start with the fact that he was notorious for his famous keynotes. He conducted training, one-on-one and in small groups. He provided free gifts. He did some miraculous product demonstrations. He did extensive networking. He had a lunch and learn. He provided coaching, counseling, community service and he was the king of content marketing. You may recall a certain book, called the Bible. Thanks to extensive research into the historicity of the New Testament writings by Lee Strobel, we know that the life of Jesus is the most documented life in the history of the ancient world. In 1995 the Bible was listed by *The Guinness Book of World Records* as having an estimated 5 billion copies sold and distributed. Today, the Bible has over 100 million copies sold or given away on average every year. Now that should give every young writer something to shoot for! Going back to my *Marketing Big Three* of brand management, sales enablement and lead generation, you can see that Jesus covered them all quite well. Best of all, you see that he used tactics that were not only effective but truly honored the buying journey of those he was called to serve. I can't emphasize how important this is for you and your organization.

What is the Greatest Marketing Tactic?

Despite all that success, there was one tactic that Jesus knew how to leverage and still stands as the greatest marketing tactic of all time. The tactic? It is word-of-mouth. There's a lot more to word-of-mouth than what you might think. Earlier we discussed the recipe for your perfect message and the power of words. We further addressed, in the messengers' chapter, how your message will be multiplied depending upon the mouth that it comes out of. When you consider the total context of tactics and methods, this elevates the concept of word-of-mouth from just an ambassador relationship management

(ARM) resource to a campaign tactic that should be deliberately developed and managed. Some of the most successful digital strategies today are largely amplified word of mouth.

Three Types of WOM

In my experience, I believe there are essentially three types of word-of-mouth. The first is what I call **WOW-WOM**. This is what happens when something so cool happens that you're compelled to tell somebody about it. Like, *Hey I just won the lottery*, or *I just got a new job*. The other type is **WHOA-WOM**. This is the compulsion to talk about something negative like, *Did you hear about that earthquake today?* Or, *Whoa, Bucky lost his leg in a tragic lawn-mower accident*! In each case, something emotional triggered a person to share it. It is this emotional driver that triggers a viral moment by compelling people to talk.

In his book, that I highly recommend, *Contagious*, Jonah Berger outlines six factors that drive people to share information and create viral movements.

- The first factor is driven by the fact that most of us will share something if it makes us look good.
- The second factor are neural triggers because something in the environment makes people think of your brand.
- The third factor is the powerful impact of emotion and how it makes you feel.
- The fourth factor is driven by visibility and do you see your product in action in the world.
- The fifth factor is the desire to share information because we think it will help people or provide practical value.
- The sixth factor is all about stories. People love to tell stories and people love to hear good stories.

Jonah Berger points out how weaving your brand within a story is a powerful gateway to making it more shareable. Jesus understood this well. By weaving strategic messages into stories, you open the door of the mind. It reminds us that we all would rather be entertained than sold something.

The Third and Worst Type of WOM

However, there is a kind of WOM that is the most hideous type possible. If you have this WOM, it's a red light on the dashboard of your marketing vehicle screaming, *Something is desperately wrong with this engine. Fix it now!* What kind of WOM is it? It's **NO-WOM**. Tragically, NO-WOM is what happens when no one is talking about your product or service offering except you. Yes, if you are the only one talking about your organization, that is a red flag. That means that you are almost doomed to be pumping the pump continuously to attract awareness and drive your marketing and sales journey. Your business can survive and even grow with this model, but you will work hard for it and it will certainly stall once you stop pumping the pump. Worst of all, it will struggle to really thrive to its full potential and offer the longevity that could be possible.

The Night to Remember at Paradise Point

Let's revisit the Paradise Point campaign. Given the likelihood that our buyer did not live in Hawaii, we decided that our best investment would be to grow our ambassador network by producing an ambassador event. It's true that we may attract some possible buyers, but our most important goal was to make our property the most talked about property on all the islands. We chose to make the event a fundraiser by partnering with a local charity. We did this for two reasons. First, it was the heart of our developer to serve this community through this charity. Second, partnering with great organizations can open the door to leaders, affluent individuals and influencers.

We may attract some possible buyers,
but our most important goal was to make
our property the most talked about
property on all the islands.

The next thing we did, right out of the messenger chapter, was to invite a celebrity, singer Roberta Flack. Many of the people from our markets' generation remember Roberta Flack as one of the greatest voices of her era so when we told people that Roberta Flack was going to be there, it became a hot ticket on the island. Not only did she add esteem, but she attracted key ambassadors, prospective buyers and opened the door to other celebrities. This eventually led to some celebrity connections including Cher, Ringo Starr and Michael J Fox.

Another thing we did was work the press. Once we had this event lined up, we had a story and that's what the press likes. We built up the home and geography as if it was a celebrity landmark. We had a story about the charity and that was newsworthy. We had a story about our special celebrity guest. This is a triple win. Important press note here: We did not simply send out a press release begging people to show up. We knew that we needed to create news to get airtime.

The last thing we did was create an experience of a lifetime. We set up a special parking area where our guests could park, and a fleet of limousines would pick them up. Once they got in the limousines, they would travel the short distance down a private road to the Paradise Point estate. As they exited their car, children from the charity would greet them with Hawaiian leis. Then, our guests would walk through the lush tropical courtyard and the luxurious great room to a stunning view of the pristine beachfront and the Mokulua Islands.

There, sitting under the palm trees was our guest, Roberta Flack, sitting at a grand piano playing Killing Me Softly. A gentle ocean breeze was our underscore as kids from the charity served a traditional Hawaiian dinner. The night was magical and when it was done, Paradise Point was the talk of the islands. Most people would consider that evening the ultimate success but remember this was an ambassador event and we didn't have our buyer quite yet. What became so exciting is that we knew how to keep a pulse on whether we had hit the mark or not. Like a Geiger counter, letting us know how close we were getting to the gold, some key metrics started kicking in and we knew something special was going to happen. We'll talk about that more in the next chapter.

Chapter 10

How Deep is Your Love?

If you can't measure it, you can't improve it.
Peter Drucker

In *The Parable of The Talents*, Jesus tells a story about a businessman who is going to leave for a while and entrusts his estate to his three servants. His first servant was given five talents from his estate. The second servant was given two talents and the last servant was given one talent. The story could easily be lost on the simplicity of a businessman leaving and entrusting his estate to three of his people. But there's a lot more going on here. At the heart of the story is a metaphor for the concept of Jesus leaving for a period of time and entrusting the well-being of his estate, or this world, to his children. Many people think of the talent metaphor as representing time, your actual talents and gifting, or your financial treasure. There's no doubt that each one of those are true assets for which we are accountable.

During the time of the story, a talent was usually a measure of some form of precious metal. I used to think it meant small coins, but a talent, if you measure by Greek standards was 26 kilograms or 57 pounds. A Roman standard would be 32 kilograms or 71 pounds. And an Egyptian talent would be 27 kilograms or 60 pounds. There was also a heavy common talent around New Testament times that weighed 130 pounds. Now that's a lot of coins! That puts the value of a talent in today's dollars as anywhere from $300,000 to $500,000.

Then the businessman returns. He's going to look to his servants and say, *Did you produce a return on investment with the resources I gave you?* To the first one, whom he gave five talents, that servant returned ten talents. To the second, whom he gave two talents, that servant returned four talents. Both of those servants provided a 100% return on investment. Then the third servant, whom he had given one talent, decided to bury it out of fear, and did not provide any return on investment. One thing that's often lost in this parable is how the businessman responds. Not only was the third servant scolded, but his talent was removed from him and given to the one who had demonstrated he could produce a return on investmnet. Whether we are talking about stewardship of this world, our time, our talents, or our financial treasures, there are two lessons that we can easily extract from this parable.

The first one is this: Whatever role we have in life, we should be accountable for delivering a meaningful outcome or return on investment. In the case of the parable the talents, 100% yield was considered a worthy return. The second lesson is this: to be accountable requires that we keep account, first an honest measure of our current or starting state, and second on the progress toward an intended outcome.

---

*Whatever role we have in life,
we should be accountable for
delivering a meaningful outcome
or return on investment.*

Strategic Metrics and Tactical Metrics

In the previous chapter, we talked about the difference between strategy and tactics. With that in mind, that also means that there is a difference between strategic goals and measurements and tactical goals and measurements. When we discussed the concept of purpose, missions, vision, values, and goals, the emphasis was to focus on your strategic goals as a company or strategic goals as a campaign or project. When we talk about tactical goals, we're really talking about the goals based upon the tactics or methodologies that you are going to use to achieve your strategic goals. All your strategic goals and their necessary metrics are going to be unique to you and your organization but let's look at a sampling of what those might be.

Financial Metrics

From an organizational standpoint it's common to have key performance indicators or KPIs for short. These are the measurements that help us track how we're doing against our goals. When considering any of these metrics, make a point of knowing what's important for your unique organization. For example, just using our P&L, we might want to measure total revenue and the sales by product category or geography. It's essential to evaluate our cost of goods and measure our expenses and review our overhead to make sure we're aligning with our goals.

This ultimately leads to our profit but that's really financial metrics 101.

Cultural Metrics

Our internal culture is critical to the success of an organization so it's valuable to measure our turnover rate and our employee satisfaction. Some people confuse the marketing voice as just a loudspeaker that projects out the front door of your business to people outside your building. If you haven't noticed, the 7DRM Strategy teaches 360-degrees of relationship. It's an integrity model. That means 360-degree love to your clients, vendors and your employees. There can be a number of reasons why an employee would choose to leave your organization, but the most common reason is leadership. There is an old saying that people don't leave organizations; they leave bad leaders. One thing we hear often is that people who don't feel loved and respected are going to walk, and you'll lose some of the greatest ambassadors for your organization.

---

*People who don't feel loved and respected
are going to walk, and you'll lose some of
the greatest ambassadors for your
organization.*

Your Customer Acquisition Cost

There are special metrics for strategic marketing objectives, and these are ones that I recommend for everybody. The first is an easy one. How many clients do you have? Is that number going up or down? The second is your customer acquisition cost. To find this, simply divide the total amount you invest to acquire customers over the course of the year. Then divide it by the number of customers you've acquired in that time. That's your customer acquisition cost or CAC for short. Whether that cost is trending up or down, it presses you to make sure that you are using your marketing resources in the most efficient and effective way.

Lifetime Value

Another marketing metric I encourage is to measure the lifetime value (LTV) of a customer. It's easy to look at how much someone spends in a week or a month or maybe a year. But when you invest in truly serving your clients and loving your clients, you will not only have raving ambassadors, but you will transform them into repeat clients, from $100 clients to $1000 clients or from $10,000 clients to $1,000,000 clients. This is the lifetime value (LTV) when a relationship produces dividends year over year over year.

When you invest in truly serving your
clients and loving your clients,
you will not only have raving
ambassadors, but you will
transform them into repeat clients.

Will Your Clients Endorse You?

The next strategic marketing metric is something called the Net Promoter Score or NPS for short. To get your NPS, use surveys to check the pulse on how likely your customers are to refer you. This is a great tool to really test, not only how well you are doing when it comes to customer retention, but it also gauges how well you are doing at transforming them into messengers or raving ambassadors. There are services you can use to assist, and you can find them online. Just search Net promoter score.

Tactical Metrics

When we turn to tactical metrics, we are measuring those things that are a part of your tactics or marketing methods. These metrics are going to be directly correlated to the methods that you decide are important for your organization. Tactical marketing metrics can be a little illusive sometimes but as we mentioned before, you can't improve what you don't monitor and measure.

For the sake of example, let's consider content marketing metrics. If you had decided that having a content marketing plan was an essential part of your marketing methods, some of the metrics would include:

1. Who is receiving and consuming my content? Are they the right market?
2. What percentage of my audience is providing email/contact data?
3. How big is my social media/email list?
4. Are those numbers increasing or decreasing?

5. What percentage of my audience is giving permission to maintain contact with them?
6. How long is my audience engaging with my material?
7. How many times is my content being shared?
8. To what degree is my audience interacting and engaging with my content?
9. To what degree do I see my audience following a recommended call to action?
10. What percentage of my audience are actually making purchases/converting?

We can't cover all the possible metrics here but remember, the actual metrics that you use are going to be tied directly to the methodology. In our coaching and workshops, we discuss this in greater detail depending on the marketing methodologies that are right for you.

Lead and Lag Metrics

It's important to note that metrics, regardless of whether they are strategic or tactical also come in two forms. There are lead metrics and there are lag metrics. The difference between a lead metric and a lag metric reminds me of when I used to work in television news. When it was time for the weather segment, the weather person would usually start with the temperatures for the last couple days. That is a lag measurement. It tells me what has already happened, but I can't really do anything about it now. It's all nice to know but it doesn't predict what will happen tomorrow. Some people try to run their organizations that way, errantly thinking that their P/L or balance sheet is a map, but like the first part of the weather forecast, a P&L can only report yesterday's news. Using these exclusively would be like trying to drive forward by looking through the rearview mirror.

On the other hand, lead metrics can be monitored to give you an indication of what tomorrow will bring. It's kind of like barometric pressure or looking out the front dash of your window. When you monitor the barometric pressure, you can see what's coming because there's a consistent pattern between the reading on that meter and whether it's going to be clear or stormy days ahead. The same holds true for your lead measurements. When you consider all the factors that may influence your desired outcomes (the lag metrics), they are not only predictive but you can now fine tune your tactics to make sure that they are producing the type of outcomes that you want to achieve, like the perfect dashboard letting you know where and when to step on the gas.

What really blew our minds was the sudden arrival of the ambassador of a lifetime! His interest would set off a world-wide frenzy that we thought would sell the home instantly.

What About Paradise Point Metrics?

When it comes to Paradise Point, we hadn't implemented a lot of methodologies. We produced videos, brochures, a website, some sales enablement resources for agents and, of course, the event experience. What we really wanted to measure were eyeballs, the true marketing equity of the 21st century. In our case, we could connect eyeballs to chatter (WOM) and this would help us build and maintain top-of-mind awareness among our ambassadors. That also meant that the metrics we used were less designed for us to do comparative analysis. We believed that the house purchase could happen fairly soon. What the metrics did was act like a Geiger counter letting us know that we were getting close to the gold and the gold was our buyer. Because we had a website, we obviously measured the traditional traffic behaviors like; How many visitors? What was the bounce rate? We wanted to know how much time they spent on the site and how many pages they viewed. This showed us the depth of interest and it was also an indicator that we were either dealing with a potential buyer, or an ambassador, such as a real estate agent, who wanted to make sure they knew their stuff in case they encountered the right buyer.

Because we had a great public relations partner, we also were looking at the number of exposures that we received in specific geographies. This allowed us to correlate the visitors to the website by geography and see where we had created the most impact with our PR spend. Of course, you can't sell a house without some showings. While it's not uncommon for a traditional buyer such as our persona/business person to look at the property, celebrities or high-profile public figures traditionally send an assistant or an agent to come visit the property on their behalf. The developer kept us in the activity loop but what really blew our minds was the sudden arrival of the ambassador of a lifetime! His interest would set off a world-wide frenzy that we thought would sell the home instantly. One metric we should have watched closer was the economy and the worst economic recession since the great depression. Navigating a business and campaign in the midst of such intense headwinds taught us some valuable lessons. We'll talk about that more in the next chapter.

Chapter 11

Havin' Babies

Anyone can count the seeds in an apple, but only God can count the number of apples in a seed.

Robert H. Schuller

When I was a boy, I had a Schwinn ten-speed bike. It was like the Rolls-Royce of bicycles in my neighborhood and I felt like I could go anywhere with it. The whole gear system fascinated me in that all I had to do was introduce a new gear with my cool handlebar gear switch and I could go faster or easier up hills while pedaling at the same pace. It was like magic!

I experienced the same fascination when they introduced moving sidewalks or people movers in airports. The feeling of taking a brisk walk (I always walk that way) but moving almost twice the speed of those poor pedestrians on the regular concourse seemed like a metaphor for life. I could multiply the distance and speed with which I moved while still walking in my regular stride if I was on the right path and using the right tools.

Be Fruitful and Multiply

Jesus referred and modeled this concept; be fruitful and multiply. To me, this is the most important discipline. While the 7DRM Strategy involves some classic disciplines that have been taught for years, if not centuries, the discipline of multiplication, hence the chapter title, Havin' Babies, is about more than growth. It's about the power of abundant growth. Just think about the word fruitful. The very essence of fruit is not only in its power to blossom, grow and nourish, but that within the seed of that fruit contains the power to make potentially millions more just like it. This so contrasts with most business models where the key is on growth, but growth through addition. While many businesses have achieved reasonable success with the addition model, the difference between checking the boxes and doing addition marketing versus leveraging the power of each discipline to produce multiplication outcomes is staggering. In this amplified marketing model, multiplication can take two basic forms: mathematical and sensory.

Multiplication by the Numbers

The first is purely mathematical. The concept premise assumes that by combining right strategies (mission, markets, messages) and tactics (methods) in harmony, we can multiply the number of impressions and potential retention in the minds of our audience. This methodology not only increases top-of-mind awareness but also triggers and satisfies a psychological need for belonging. *Heck- everyone is buying this product so it's safe, accepted and maybe even validating to be seen with this brand.*

The other mathematical model is the M.A.P. model. This is where we multiply through mergers, acquisitions and partnerships. Note, I said multiply. You can conduct the same behaviors to add to your business, but the very best is when the combination actually multiplies opportunities, opens new markets, provides a multiple on the ability to do R&D, release products and accelerate revenue growth. This must become a mindset and it will soon separate good opportunities from great opportunities.

*Sensory multiplication is powerful
because it leverages the power of emotion
and the sweet intoxication that comes
when our brain produces dopamine.*

Multiplication by the Senses

Sensory multiplication is powerful because it leverages the power of emotion and the sweet intoxication that comes when our brain produces dopamine. When you implement messengers and ambassadors, we can induce that connection because it is a natural byproduct of genuine connection with people. When you can look into the eyes of a brand ambassador, a heightened level of engagement begins because we not only have great words coming out of an esteemed or celebrated mouth (WOW-WOM), you get the multiplying factor of being cradled by the gentle fragrance of good feelings like trust, caring, honesty, authenticity. This is power and you want it attached to your brand!

The Multiplying Power of Experiences

Sensory multiplication explodes when we produce powerful experiences. Remember our discussion of post-traumatic growth and the Paradise Point experience? How about when you met that special someone? Your first kiss? When a child was born? As long as those experiences were not clouded by a tragic breakup, you get what I mean. Strategically creating powerful experiences are a strategic key to exploding a brand impression that will repeat in your markets mind over and over and can last a lifetime.

> *Strategically creating powerful experiences are a strategic key to exploding a brand impression that will repeat in your markets mind over and over and can last a lifetime.*

Quick tip: If your market does not respond with wow, keep working at it. You missed the mark. It's one thing to be inspired by the work of others, but if you copied someone else's style or model or method, that is probably why no one said *wow*. It's just me-too marketing, and that's been done before. I hope that wasn't too harsh. This is some advance material that I usually save for our workshops but let me give you a very quick insight. Recall when I mentioned that most buyer decisions are driven by pleasure and pain with pain being the dominant motivator. A similar scenario exists for many business owners. When they are making marketing decisions, they are most commonly driven by faith and fear with fear being the dominant motivator. Since business owners don't want to make mistakes, look stupid, take too many risks, they just do what they did before or mimic what they see others doing. It's similar to what happens in the motion picture industry. The prospect of taking a risk on doing something real, fresh, insightful, ground-breaking and honest might sound appealing, but the fear of failure and rejection causes many studios to copy each other, to try to do remakes, sequels, and play it safe. Sadly, that's what many businesses do every day.

The Multiplying Power of Brand Harmony

A comprehensive branding strategy is another sensory opportunity to leverage the discipline of multiplication. When most people think of branding, they often associate it with logos, typefaces, layouts and colors. However, complete branding should include all sensory experiences including sight, sound, smell, taste, and when possible, touch. When you combine these elements with a missional and value driven culture, meaningful messages, product experiences and style, we introduce the more powerful multiplication of brand experiences by creating a living brand personality. At this point we enter into the exciting realm of bringing your brand to life in such a manner that it almost becomes human. You feel like you know, like and trust it. A well-developed brand can become your friend, something that brings value to you, your life and you feel good about associating with it. In fact, you want people to know that you associate with it because the brand has the attributes we either embody or aspire to.

A well-developed brand can become your friend, something that brings value to you, your life and you feel good about associating with.

Re-Engaging the Senses

When it comes to branding, one of the points that is missed by so many, including so-called branding experts, is that, at its best, it starts to pay psychological dividends when we are re-engaging human senses to reattach indelible thoughts and feelings with your organization. For example, many people still look at the traditional TV ad format as the king of branding. Whether you see it online or offline, the format is classic. In fact, once a year, millions of people around the world gather around their TV's with friends and family to celebrate this most coveted artform. We call this the Super Bowl. Oh yes, there is some football being played as relief between commercials. For many people, they mistakenly observe this artform as a vehicle for awareness as if you've never heard of **NIKE** or Coke or Budweiser or Doritos. It's true that there may be one or two commercials that are rolling the dice on the big game to have their coming out party. However, the real game is re-awareness. What we have are established brands that have decided to make an exclamation point on an already established brand message or personality. And if they can induce an *awe* or *whoa* or *holy crap* or a laugh, you might hit the viral sharing lottery. Their brand exposures now explode along with the hopeful good feelings (dopamine) that comes with making someone feel special for sharing. If people don't understand this, they will make the tragic mistake of mimicking the behavior at a smaller level without the strategic drivers and context to make it effective. That's not only bad marketing, it's really bad business because it wastes so much money, and marketing, of course, will get the blame for it. This is a good time to point out that this is also a form of me-too marketing in that a business owner watches what someone else does and tries to mimic it without any strategic context. There is another book here, but I will save the deeper discussion for another time, or you can ask in a coaching session or workshop. I hope you can see how exciting this can be for your organization. If a Rabbi/Small Businessman from Nazareth can apply these disciplines, so can you! I believe he said something about you doing greater things…

> *Every single touchpoint with your organization will either build and multiply your brand or it will undermine it.*

No Silver Bullets

In honoring the discipline of multiplication, there is no silver bullet. Being strategic, vigilant and proactive is an important difference between fundamental marketing and launching movements. That's why we encourage organizations to pay close attention to every detail of their internal and external engagements. Every single touchpoint with your organization will either build and multiply your brand or it will undermine it.

Don't take lightly every experience that touches your market. Be careful to express and live your brand to every vendor, partner or employee by practicing 360-degree love. This is called brand integrity, the term we get from math meaning whole number, integer. It means we aren't two-faced but true to our aspiration and values everywhere and all the time.

Multiplication by Associative/Engrafting Brands

With true multiplication, we can leverage another power of fruitfulness. Just as Jesus modeled elements of the M.A.P, model through partnerships (with his ambassador/disciples) and the acquisition (with John the Baptist) multiplication emerges in yet, another form called engrafting (or the ultimate merger). This is an age-old method of attaching one type of branch to another branch to produce types of fruit and quantities of fruit that would not otherwise exist by themselves. The model is both profound and amazingly practical in nature as could be with your organization. Just honor the total 7DRM Strategy and you will have built the foundation for incredible success.

> *Honor the total 7DRM Strategy and you will have built the foundation for incredible success.*

Paradise Point: We were blown away!

I mentioned that we were blown away with what unfolded with Paradise Point so let's start with a little review:

1. We were clear about our purpose, missions and vision for the campaign.
2. We did our homework, used the 10-Digit Human Address and developed a highly desirable target market that would provide the highest likelihood for selling the property.
3. We crafted a core message by using the ultimate brand message recipe of weaving our strategic

outcomes with the WINOFF insights of our target market.

4. We structured an ambassador relationship management (ARM) plan to acquire key, influential ambassadors and compel them to share.

5. We incorporated some traditional marketing tactics (website, brochures, videos) for sales enablement but added the experiential marketing gala that produced massive amounts of marketing gold (WOW-WOM) that kept our ambassadors buzzing.

Not Our Perfect Story

If this were a perfect story, I'd wrap this up by saying that the next day, we received a call from one of the local agents and he had a buyer ready to sign. That didn't happen. Did our system not work? Did we miss something? No! The 7DRM Strategy is a marketing system that is still subject to market conditions, timing and the most unpredictable aspect of business, people. If you are confident that you are doing the right things, then you must be patient and honor the process. It can look like baking. After all the mixing and stirring is done, the most complex sales still take time and you have to let it bake. But... it didn't bake for long. No, we didn't get the immediate buyer, but we did get to add one more ingredient, one of the best ambassadors you could ever hope for. You think our gala experiences sounded magical, they took a back seat to what happened next.

This whole episode happened right around the time that a certain Hawaiian native was elected President of the United States.

The Better Perfect Story

This whole episode happened right around the time that a certain Hawaiian native was elected president of the United States. He had decided that to celebrate, he would take his family to his childhood home of Hawaii and start an annual tradition. When his team reached out to friends and business associates in Hawaii, they had a great recommendation; Paradise Point, of course. After a series of discussions with the secret service to validate the celebrity-level security and the suitability for the First Family, the deal was done, and President-elect Obama was going to spend the holidays at Paradise Point. When the president-elect arrived, we received some great press and interest started percolating for the property. But this also came during the dawn of the great recession. The president came and left. We really thought this would sell the home. We watched in wonder as this tidal wave of exposure rolled in but then, like a Hawaiian tide, watched in horror as the wave gently washed back out to sea. Our client rented out the property for a season while our ideal target market was sitting on the sidelines, waiting to see what would happen with the economy before they made any giant investments. Six months passed before we received another call from the White House asking if the home could be available for First Family. My client said yes and this time, we were ready to step up our ambassador game. Cue the *Rocky* theme!

We launched an ambassador/tactical plan that would not only honor the security of the First Family but take our brand into the stratosphere.

If Any Plane Can Become Air Force One...

One of the tough aspects of getting this particular ambassador is that we have to keep it a secret, at least until he is just about to arrive. The flurry of security and extensive preparations tend to give a lot of the story away. But we launched an ambassador/tactical plan that would not only honor the security of the First Family but take our brand into the stratosphere.

Step One: Leverage our ambassador to elevate the brand. Living next to and having worked with NIKE, I've seen them master the practice of associative or engrafted branding. While NIKE makes great shoes, nothing has been more powerful as when they attached their brand (engrafting) to the great Michael Jordan. They were smart! They didn't just show Michael wearing NIKE shoes, they took it to the next step and developed the Air Jordan, a powerful brand that still thrives today. With that in mind, did you know that the minute the President of the United States steps on virtually any plane, it is immediately designated Air Force One? We took that to heart, and rebranded Paradise Point as the Obama Winter White House.

Step Two: Rebrand all resources and maximize SEO to drive traffic for Obama Winter White House to our sites.

Step Three: Reach out to my associates at ABC and *Good Morning America (GMA)*. Since I had a connection with ABC, I felt confident that we could establish a mutually beneficial plan that we could all keep confidential until just the right moment. I first considered what they would want, since I had lived in that world for so long. We agreed to a network TV exclusive. We agreed they would be first with the story. We would arrange complete access to the property before the arrival of the First Family. All would be cleared with the Secret Service. It helped that I had a secret service file and an old clearance from my broadcast days so we understood how delicate this could be. Knowing that once something airs on *Good Morning America*, it's going to be shared on *World News Tonight* (WNT) and probably dozens of entertainment programs like *Entertainment Tonight* across the country. This was a hot story and we were going to control the origin and timing of airing. Oh, and one last thing. Since we know that everything that is aired will also be transcribed and hit the web in hundreds of locations world-wide, we asked that, whether it was in the introduction, body of the story or post-story wrap, they needed to say Obama Winter White House multiple times.

This was a hot story and we were going to control the origin and timing of airing.

Step Four: Leading up to this time, we had considered traditional advertising, but we just couldn't justify the expenditure that would hit our target market. For example, one of the great premium magazines featuring high-end beach front property is *Ocean Home Magazine*. They are a stunning publication and their owner is hands-on and cares about every little detail. I liked and respected them so much, but I honestly felt bad that it never was quite the right situation to do business. Then, the Obama Winter White House landed in our lap. Knowing that we were about to go national just before Christmas, I thought of the perfect present for *Ocean Home Magazine* and my client. We would offer the publication the exclusive print opportunity to the story. We negotiated the deal in 72 hours and, for just the cost of our brilliant photographer, we were able to feature the Obama Winter White House on the cover of the magazine and in a gorgeous multi-page spread right in the center.

Step Five: Prepare a media plan. With this much press, we needed to be prepared for the demand for information or resources. Fortunately, we had a beautifully pre-crafted message about the property and video resources. We typically call this a **PR Reel** because it hand-picks all the images you would like to have seen about your story and the press loves it because you do most of the work for them. Of course, in this case, they could not have access to the property while the First Family was staying there so our video was the next best thing. Also note, once ABC aired their story, we could share the story with anyone in the world now.... and we did.

Even today, if you search
Obama Winter White House, the effort
we invested into honoring
the 7DRM Strategy and empowering
our ambassadors pays dividends in
impact and longevity to the brand.

Just before Christmas, the story aired and was repeated hundreds of times over the next couple months. Simply by revisiting the 7DRM strategy, we had leveraged the moment and transformed it into another experiential windfall by sheer number of eyes that were impacted.

(As a special gift, if you'd like to see the magazine layout and the Good Morning America story, just go to www.7DRM.com/eastereggs.)

Despite being deep into the Great Recession, interest started to percolate. We didn't even need our target market to have seen any of the press coverage. Once they would inquire about beach-front property, we knew the Obama Winter White House would become a part of the discussion because our island ambassadors had seen the coverage and may have even attended our gala. And it worked. Even today, if you search Obama Winter White House, the effort we invested into honoring the 7DRM Strategy and empowering our ambassadors pays dividends in impact and longevity to the brand. Best of all, we found our buyer and curiously, he fit very closely to the persona we had developed for him. He is a great guy and while he will rent it out to a select few, he loves bringing his friends, family and business associates to his estate. In fact, he loves having his family there over the holidays so much that when the White House inquired about returning, he turned them down. As he put it to me, his family is more important than the President to him.

Now that you have seen every one of the 7 Disciplines in action, I'd like to give you a model that will help you remember and share with your teams. In all my coaching and workshops with clients, what I'm about to share in the next chapter is one of the most popular and it will put it all together for you so that you can start applying the 7 Disciplines today.

Chapter 12

Putting It All Together

Follow me and I will make you fishers of men.
Jesus Christ

I mentioned earlier that after my death experience, I began a much deeper spiritual journey. This included re-reading the works by the great philosophers such as Plato, Socrates and Aristotle. I hadn't read them since college. I discovered some great perspectives about Jesus from Muslim authors and the great Jewish historian, Josephus. But obviously, the largest treasure chest about Jesus is contained in the works of Matthew, Mark, Luke and John. Not that I was skeptical, but my Jesuit Catholic roots demanded that I dig deeper as to the origins of these writings. I was shocked!

While I still regularly quote and appreciate the words of Plato, Socrates and Aristotle, I found it fascinating that the time elapsed between the original writing and any copies of those writings was over 1000 years. And in the case of Plato, only some 250 copies of manuscripts of his writings have been discovered. In contrast, the lapsed time between origin and any copy of New Testament writings is as early as 29 years (a fragment from the Gospel of John) and there is a total supporting New Testament manuscript base of over 24,000 documents. What was even more impressive is that these manuscripts agree completely 99.5% of the time. That gave me an enormous level of confidence that I wasn't reading some fairytale, but genuine cross-referenced historical documents that would give me real insight into the words and actions of this person named Jesus.

What was even more impressive is that these manuscripts agree completely 99.5% of the time.

Fishers of Men

One of the earliest texts tells the story of Jesus when he began preaching in Galilee. As he approached two fishermen, Simon Peter and Andrew, he called out to them and said, *Follow me, and I will make you fishers of men.* This was a little unusual for a Rabbi at that time because, while a Rabbi would often have followers, his followers usually pursued the Rabbi. In this case, Jesus pursued the fishermen. Another thing worth noting is that while most translations use the term men, the original Greek was gender neutral meaning everybody. For centuries, theologians have taught about the profound spiritual metaphor that exists in this simple invitation. I found this simple invitation, to become fishers of men, to be powerful because in it lies, the foundational principles that are contained in the 7DRM strategy.

I found this simple invitation, to become fishers of men, to be powerful because in it lies, the foundational principles that are contained in the 7DRM strategy.

I have never been much of a fisherman, but I do know this much, if I were ever to go fishing again, I'd have to ask, *Why am I fishing?* That's a great question and it is a mission driven question. The next natural question to ask is, *What are you fishing for?* That's a market question. The next question might be, *Where will I find these fish (lake, river, ocean)?* That's a great demographic-driven question. If

I'm a thoughtful and prepared strategic fisherman, I'd would ask, *What are they biting on?* That's a message question. Sometimes people fish alone but most of the time, they travel in groups or even use guides. If I wanted to know, *Who will be my fishing partners?* that's a messenger/ambassador question. Then of course, depending upon the answers to all these questions, the next natural question might be, *What tools am I going to use?* In other words, *What kind of pole and hook and line weight will I use?* Or, *Am I going to use a net? Will I fish from a boat and go to the fish or will I fish from a dock and hope that they come to me?* These are actually method (and business model) questions. And if I'm actually any good, (and I have never personally asked this question while fishing), *What's the limit?* That's really a metrics question.

By living the Fishers of Men model, essentially the 7DRM Strategy, you are living your brand through the transformation of your culture and the manner in which you love, respect and honor your markets.

When you apply the Fishers of Men concept to marketing, there is a lot of comparisons that simply make sense. For example, asking what they're biting on leads to the formation of your hook, your core message. Sometimes, like the famous scene out of the movie *Jaws*, you may need to churn the waters to attract the fish to you. By living the Fishers of Men model, essentially the 7DRM Strategy, you are living your brand through the transformation of your culture and the manner in which you love, respect and honor your markets. This makes the fish (your market) attracted to you and want to be connected to you whether it be at a dock (fixed location) or in a boat (a dynamic or virtual location where you can take your product direct to the end-user). Next, you have to be strategic about the real buying journey that the fish (your market) makes from the encounter with a hook to actually getting in the boat with you.

The Buying Journey

As a practice for trying to know our markets, we earlier discussed the traditional buying journey. Bringing that to life in this example, you create **awareness** when the fish becomes aware of the bait triggering the reticular activating system that says that something you are offering is relevant. The next step from awareness is to move to the **learning** stage. That's the gathering of information stage that reinforces that, in fact, what they thought was interesting should be pursued further. The next is the **understanding** stage. The understanding stage is a critical intersection of decision. This is where the buyer makes, an often, split-second decision that either you are a viable solution to their problem, or you are not. If you are not a viable solution, the journey stops, and you are dismissed. If, on the other hand, your market determines that you are a viable solution, you are **embraced**, and the journey continues. From this stage, you are usually just details away from moving to the next stage where you and your solution receive **buy-in**. If this is not a complex sale or there is a heightened sense of urgency, you move swiftly to **action** and the purchase. However, if this follows the traditional complex sale in the corporate world or in larger non-profits, there may be hoops to jump through including getting the CFO approval, getting feedback from a committee, or your prospects need to release another vendor that is currently managing that account. This process can last 10 seconds to 10 months depending on the complexity of the product, the process of your market, and the number of people involved with approving the decision. Don't be discouraged, these are real processes but if you navigate these deliberately, they will be joining you in the boat soon!

The Jesus model of marketing is not a catch and keep model.
It is a catch and release model.

Catch and Release

For most businesses, they start celebrating and doing the victory dance in the end zone because they made the sale. For many businesses and organizations this is where it stops. But that is not the 7DRM Strategy. It's not the Jesus model of marketing. The Jesus model of marketing is not a catch and keep model. It is a catch and release model. The goal, once you have them in the boat, is to give them such a profound experience that they transform from simple clients or customers to raving ambassadors. At that point, they are released back into the marketplace to their spheres of influence where they will be your ambassadors to attract your next group of clients.

What's incredibly powerful about that process is instead of having to go through the full cycle of awareness and learning and understanding, they bypass all those stages because they have now received a powerful endorsement from an esteemed authority in their life and it moves them immediately to the embrace stage. From that point, it's just a matter of getting a deeper understanding of the breadth and depth of their needs and to see if they are a good fit for your product or services.

This is one of the reasons that Jesus ministry exploded. It was this 7DRM catch and release model, empowered by one of the most effective methodologies of marketing in the history of mankind, word-of-mouth. Study after study continues to support that of all forms of marketing and advertising, recommendations from people we know retain the highest trust level at over 80%. That places it way ahead of virtually any other form of advertising including website, social media, television, newspaper, magazines, product placement, radio or movies, just to name a few. What this does is place a significant weight on your product experience. In other words, deliver and keep your promises to truly love and serve your client. Your integrity and the well-being of your organization is at stake. The bottom line is this when you honor the 7DRM Strategy, you are deliberate and thoughtful because you love and serve your market, and this is the most efficient model for honoring the buying journey. What you also did was create momentum, the kind of momentum that is the birthplace of movements.

When you honor the 7DRM Strategy, you are deliberate and thoughtful because you love and serve your market, and this is the most efficient model for honoring the buying journey.

Relationships Take Work

As excited as I am about this system and as successful as it has been through history, the biggest obstacle is the fact that relationships take work. It's not uncommon for marketing teams to be lured into simply managing those relationships instead of helping them flourish and thrive. We've all seen what happens to relationships that are reduced to management. Not to say that your client relationships are as demanding as a marriage, but even these most sacred relationships fail over half the time because, in part, sometimes they slide into problem solving and management mode. This not only weakens the relationship, but it makes it very hard for your team. Instead of being proactive to help the relationship grow and flourish, your team is usually only addressing the client when there is a problem to solve. These relationships are doomed to failure. Your customer service team suddenly looks forward to Friday because they can escape a culture of having to manage painful relationships and putting out fires instead of celebrating the sweet victories of delivering an exceptional customer experience.

Don't Try to Do it Alone

If it really is your desire to transform your culture into a vibrant 7DRM business, then I encourage you to get the support you need to establish those foundational strategic initiatives. Get clear on your purpose, your missions and crafting a compelling vision that is so crystal clear, people are not consumed by distraction but can paddle together with the absolute clarity of where they are going and why they want to go there. Help them understand and live your values and let them see the goals so that they can work with you to advance towards them and see them realized. Help your team understand your market and to know it intimately. Remove all the questions and get rid of the fog of crafting messages that are written to everybody but really are to nobody because they are not targeted or meaningful. Help your team be strategic about opportunities to build an army of ambassadors whether that be with your vendors, strategic partners, joint ventures, but most important, with every single customer that comes through your door. Then help them see how the methodologies that you use to advance your marketing are not just checkboxes because everybody else is doing it.

> *Having a framework of thinking about multiplication where you're not just thinking about growth but abundant growth in all areas will help you create a culture of excitement.*

Your team will see the harmony and the power and the purpose behind every methodology to accelerate the buyer journey and to build a brand culture that is going to help you grow and flourish. Lastly measure and multiply. Having a framework of thinking about multiplication where you're not just thinking about growth but abundant growth in all areas will help you create a culture of excitement. Imagine what it would be like if your people came to work every day because they have a purpose and missions to accomplish that will help them realize their greatest hopes and dreams.

Three Key Ingredients for Your Success

We find that when any organization wants to truly make a profound difference or tackle a major initiative, they need three key ingredients. The first is expertise. What you have in this book is a framework for what it takes to execute a 7DRM strategy but if you've never done it before, it can be difficult to navigate. There are going to be times that you're going to reach intersections and questions and there can be real value in having strategic support to walk you through the process with someone who has done it before.

> *Objectivity plays a critical role in helping organizations see themselves more clearly.*

The next ingredient is objectivity. When you're inside your business, it's easy to miss the details. Like the old saying goes, being able to tell the difference between the forest and the trees. Here in Portland, NIKE has had a rich relationship with one of the greatest advertising agencies in the world, *Wieden and Kennedy*. W&K is responsible for some of the most famous advertising campaigns like Old Spice, Coca-Cola and of course, the Just Do It campaign for NIKE. From purely a financial perspective, NIKE could probably buy W&K with pocket change. But what we see is that objectivity plays a critical role in helping organizations see themselves more clearly. NIKE values the objectivity that comes from an organization that eats and breathes advertising, that works in a diverse marketing culture, and experiences the latest in strategies, tactics and trends. Leveraging objectivity allows NIKE to look at its organization with fresh eyes. That objectivity is priceless.

Let's face it, your people work hard every day and it's very likely that they're not sitting idly waiting for another task to be plopped on their plate.

The last ingredient is capacity. Let's face it, your people work hard every day and it's very likely that they're not sitting idly waiting for another task to be plopped on their plate. Implementing a 7DRM Strategy does take time and to do that, we have found that companies often need capacity support. Sometimes, it's to provide strategic coaching. Sometimes it's to provide ongoing consulting to walk an organization through the process and hold them accountable. Sometimes, it's to lead the entire training and implementation process from top to bottom.

What I experienced the day I crossed the threshold of eternity, changed my life forever.

The Choice is Yours

Now that you understand the framework for a 7DRM strategy, the choice is yours. Are you ready to move forward to help transform your culture and your organization to be the very best it can be? When you started this book, I shared just a little about my death experience and how it launched me on this journey to discover the 7DRM strategy. What I experienced the day I crossed the threshold of eternity, changed my life forever. In the next chapter, I'd like to get personal and share with you, the rest of that story.

Chapter 13

Today is Your Launch Day

*Every person has a longing to be significant;
to make a contribution; to be a part
of something noble and purposeful.*

John Maxwell

Today, as I write this last chapter of *The 7 Disciplines of Relationship Marketing*, I actually have tears in my eyes. It's been an extraordinary journey and one for which I am incredibly thankful. The journey has been like all our journeys, filled with hopes, dreams, adventure and disappointments. However, this week is particularly special as I celebrate my 20th re-birthday. Yes, it's been 20 years since I lost my life and my life was given back to me. I try never to take that for granted and I am still learning and processing everything I experienced. One thing I must stress. I am not a theologian. I am a husband, father and media guy. My experience is not intended to define or confirm any theology but instead, to simply share my deeply personal experience with you. I am honored that you are reading this so that I can share it with you.

I lived and believed that everything revolved around the media circus but there is a wise proverb that paraphrased, states, 'pride goes before the fall.' I was ripe for a fall.

Pride Comes Before the Fall

When I reflect on that day when I boarded that plane to Nashville, I could never have imagined what I was about to experience. As I mentioned earlier, I was on my way to sign a contract for a documentary distribution deal and I thought I was on top of the world. I had worked for so many years directing TV, corporate events and large-scale entertainment with some giant names, but this was different. I was about to be paid an advance for a documentary that could be the first of dozens with our production company. This could be really big, and that was about the size of my head. I was full of myself. It scares me how distracted I was by the media circus. I lived and believed that everything revolved around the media circus but there is a wise proverb that paraphrased, states, pride goes before the fall. I was ripe for a fall.

As I mentioned earlier in the book, I wasn't feeling physically well that morning. This was crazy because I never get sick but this day, I really felt strange. When I felt convinced that something was about to happen, about 40 minutes into the flight, I turned to Timothy, and told him something wasn't right. That fast, my eyes rolled back in my head. My arms fell limp by my sides, and my heart stopped. I've been known to joke from time-to-time, but this was no joke.

Crossing the Threshold of Eternity

In the blink of an eye, I crossed the threshold into eternity. I use that term because I literally felt a difference between moving from a dimension of time to a dimension of no time, at least as we know it. I know there's lots of people who have had similar experiences who describe pearly gates, golden streets and choirs of angels. I had none of those. The peace I felt was both deafening and shocking. It was if a laser beam pierced through the top of my head and I instantly understood things I never understood at any time in my life or could hope to. I'd say it was mind blowing but it was completely spiritual so I can't say that my mind was doing a lot of processing. That would happen after I returned.

I was terrified of coming
face-to-face with God.

I Didn't Want to Meet God

I should let you know that growing up, deep down inside, I was terrified of coming face-to-face with God. Because of painful experiences I had and the culture I was raised in, I believed that if I ever came face-to-face with God, he'd be pissed at me. Instead of getting a warm hug, I was going to get a finger pointed in my face. Then God would yell about every place that I screwed up or did something wrong. I'd be called names and ridiculed for all my shortcomings and all my failures. The picture I had painted in my mind felt more like an encounter with the Wizard of Oz when he was yelling at Dorothy, but I would never have her courage to confront the attacks. I never wanted to meet the Oz-God!

It Wasn't What I Expected

In a letter that Paul of Tarsus wrote to the believers in Ephesus, he prayed that they would be rooted and grounded in love, and that they could comprehend the breadth, length, depth and height of God's love. It sounds nice enough to read and might make a good wall plaque, but I really got it! Seriously! I finally got it! Instead of the Oz-God, I came face-to-face with the total and complete embodiment of love! In being in the presence of God, I was present with complete love itself. What was equally staggering was that the love was eternal as God is eternal. When Paul talked about the breadth, length, depth and height of God's love, what was really being revealed it that there is no way to measure it, find it's limit in any form because God's love is as infinite and eternal as God is infinite and eternal.

> *God did not manifest in a human form but instead was all encompassing, consuming me 360 degrees with his presence and overwhelming love.*

God did not manifest in a human form but instead was all encompassing, consuming me 360 degrees with his presence and overwhelming love. There are a lot of ways our world describes God. We usually reference attributes like just, merciful, faithful, trustworthy, patient, kind and loving, just to name a few. However, it was clear to me that while all these attributes are real, they are not separate attributes but expressions of God that flow out of his love. It should be no surprise that John, the one who referred to himself as the one Jesus loved, wrote that *God is love.*

As God's love engulfed me all around, I felt so close, so cared for, so known, but then a sudden awareness pierced my heart. This one thing alone, brings me so much peace, hope and trust in God and you need to know this. God doesn't just love you, God is madly in love with you! Please absorb that for a minute. God cares about your every dream and every hope. God feels every one of your tears, fears, hurts and doubts with you. God has been with you through every season of your life and has experienced every detail because God is the embodiment of eternal love and is so madly in love with you. Now I get it. God asks us to love him with all our heart and soul and mind and strength because that's how much God loves us. It is the perfect completion of the perfect relationship.

God doesn't just love you,
God is madly in love with you!

Another unexpected yet profound realization is the recognition of no time. I had a clear sense that once I crossed the threshold of eternity, everything that has happened or will happen, has happened. Despite the time that was passing as Timothy was trying to resuscitate me on a plane somewhere over the Midwest, from my experience I couldn't tell you if I was away for 5 minutes or 5 million years. In eternity there's really no difference but it was time to come back.

My journey back was perhaps a little less spiritual and more physiological. Some have described it as the brain rebooting as you resume conscious thought and your body begins to function again. Imagine having every scene from your life, frozen into thousands of still pictures. Then, imagine every one of those pictures cut into hundreds of pieces like a puzzle and thrown into the air in front of a giant fan. I sensed that I was moving forward at an ever-increasing speed and as fragmented scenes of my life blew by me, I was both familiar yet frustrated that I could not gather all the context of the scene. The pieces accelerated flying faster and faster and faster. I couldn't tell now if I was going towards them or they were coming at me. As they peaked at a blur of maximum velocity, I suddenly opened my eyes. I was back. Then it struck me that while the other side is so lovingly majestic and overwhelming, it was also so peaceful. When I opened my eyes in the plane, I re-entered a world that seemed chaotic and intensely loud by comparison.

We Are Given a Gift Everyday

Every day since, I look at life differently. I'm not only reminded of a God who is madly in love with me but that I was given a gift. And it's a gift that we all get every day. You see, the idea of waking up, opening our eyes in the morning and getting out of bed to start our day isn't something I think any of us have ever really earned or deserve. I believe it's a gift from God, and it's a gift with a love note. The love note simply says:

Good morning!

I am madly in love with you!

I've given you another day because you
have a powerful purpose to fulfill and
many lives to touch. My gift of breath to
you today is a confirmation of my
complete love for you. I now ask that you
love me back the way I love you, love all
the lives I have put within your world
and love yourself in order to live
the joy and fulness of your purpose.

Today is Your Launch Day

The morning of my death, I had no idea what I was about to encounter and what might lie ahead. Since then, we've experienced opportunities I could have never imagined. We have been able to touch millions of lives in the corporate, entertainment and non-profit worlds and we've been able to identify and practice the 7DRM Strategy. Other than receiving the gift of life, perhaps what I am most thankful for is that despite my believing and praying for my Plan A to manifest in my life, God chose to answer my prayer with his Plan B, as in Plan Blessed. His ways are truly greater than my ways and I was not prepared to dream or believe at his level. I hope now that you can. *The 7 Disciplines of Relationship Marketing* is not just a marketing strategy but a beautiful roadmap, a way of life that, when applied not only will provide profitable returns but will build the foundation for your ongoing legacy. This is a legacy that will not just be built and measured in a bank account, but a legacy that will be measured in lives impacted. This is a legacy that is built in the most profound way possible, with the love of God.

I am praying for you and we are here for you. Remember that countdown- 10, 9, 8, 7, 6, 5, 4, 3, 2, 1. Today is your launch day! And I'm honored to be a part of your journey!

Acknowledgements

Anyone who has accomplished anything of any significance, ultimately faces the fact that no one is self-made. In a book that emphasizes the power and need for meaningful relationships, it's no surprise that I have a long list of people for whom I owe a debt of gratitude. The following people have encouraged me, influenced me, taught me, corrected me, tolerated me, but ultimately loved me. It is with a spirit of love and gratitude that I simply thank you!

Thank you to my incredibly gifted Spirit Media Family who partnered with me through the years to inspire this book and help make a difference in this world: C. Jeffrey Abbott, Kelly Anderson, Anne DeRock, Willy Dolan, Don Eck, Dan Elsner, Zee Farrouge, Brian Gage, Timothy Greenidge, Kevin Hart, Kathleen Kelly, Jean Klewitz, Tim Law, Steve Meyer, Jennifer Morrison, Tim Neill, Jessica Parsons, Scott Pelot, Kate Rurik, Ricky Russ, Jr., Suzanne Shelley, Grant Shirahama, Warren Shultz, TC Smith, David Spangler, Cathy Wegrzyn, and Patty Wisner.

Thank you to the circle of great men in my life who have challenged me, kicked me in the butt and held me accountable to make this second chance at life matter: Brad Biegert, Larry Briggs, Ron Carlson, Randy Carr, Dave Chin, Rod Cummings, Terry Deming, Ron Frey, Mark Green, Craig Holiday, Steve Jones, Ken Kirkwood, Gordon Lundquist, Steve Mueller, Bob Ochs, Robb Pickens, Randy Sanford, Allan Schrader, Eugene Wallace, Allan Wich and David Zimel.

Thank you to the influencers who I have had either the pleasure of meeting, working with or simply inspired me to use my voice to promote hope, healing, understanding and the love of God to this world: Stephen Baldwin, Ken Blanchard, Jonah Berger, Larry Burkett, Terence Chatmon, Robert Cialdini, President William Clinton, Milo O. Frank, Michael E. Gerber, Malcolm Gladwell, Seth Godin, Dean Graziosi, Darren Hardy, Daniel Harkavy, Kevin Harrington, Todd Hunter, Michael Hyatt, Robert Kiyosaki, Dr. Angela E. Lauria, Dr. Carolina Leaf, Jen Limm, P. Griff Lindell, John Maxwell, Ora North, Luis Palau, Charlie Plumb, Dolores Preble, Tony Robbins, Jim Rohn, Beverly Sallee, Dr. Jack

Schafer, Steve K. Scott, Simon Sinek, Lee Strobel, Ford Taylor, Dennis Waitley, Rick Warren, Jim White, Roy H. Williams and William P. Young.

Finally, and above all, thanks to God for giving me the breath today to share this story.

About the Author

William Dolan is President and Creative Director of Spirit Media, a creative marketing agency based in Portland, Oregon. As an Emmy-nominated Producer and Director, William has been a part of producing live events for 500 to 250,000 people, directed national and international TV broadcasts for millions, and has acted as creative consultant for hundreds of organizations, from emerging small businesses to Fortune 500 companies. His extensive background in media and entertainment led him to collaborating with or directing many noted celebrities including Gwen Stefani, The Black Eyed Peas, Maroon 5, Kenny Chesney, President Bill Clinton, Alec Baldwin and hundreds more in the fields of business, sports, ministry, entertainment and politics.

In 1999, William had a near-death experience that dramatically challenged his view of life, his career path, and the fields of communication and marketing. Years of research and application led him to the discovery of The 7 Disciplines of Relationship Marketing (the 7DRM Strategy). Today, William shares the 7DRM Strategy through online and live workshops, individual coaching and through the marketing services offered through his creative agency, Spirit Media. William has also shared his insights as a keynote or workshop leader for the National Association of Broadcasters, The National Christian Leadership Alliance, the American Marketing Association and various universities and business groups around the United States.

William has been married to his high-school sweetheart, Camilla, for over 30 years. They have five incredible adult children, one beautiful daughter-in-law and (in their words) the two most adorable grandchildren in the world. Their family also includes several grand pets including his writing companion, Marcella, his attention-starved tabby cat. When William isn't working with clients or having time with family and friends, you'll find him either working out, hiking the neighborhood mountain or experimenting in the kitchen trying to refine his latest oatmeal-chocolate chip cookie recipe.

Thank you. I have a gift for you!

It means the world to me that you read, and I hope enjoyed, *The 7 Disciplines of Relationship Marketing.* Applying the 7DRM Strategy takes some time and work but it is life-changing.   So, whether you are developing your business, refining your business or needing to do a complete overhaul of your marketing system, we are here for you and I'm praying for you!

If you have a question, concerns or would like to learn about how you can sign up for our free VLOG, learn about upcoming workshops or arrange a coaching call, go to www.7DRM.com.

As a special gift for reading this book, I mentioned a couple surprises just for you. One is from the Paradise Point story where I will share with you some of the media resources that we developed in partnership with our magazine publisher and our friends at ABC-TV.

The next special gift is a training that will walk you through the ultimate message recipe. This is a great teaching and will help add understanding as you work to develop or refine your perfect message. It's also a preview of an online workshop coming soon that your entire team can study and apply. These gifts are absolutely free, and you will find them both at www.7DRM.com/eastereggs.

Again, thank you! It is my honor to have shared these powerful disciplines with you. I pray that they will help transform your business, your culture and you!

With much Love and Appreciation-
William J. Dolan

Further Reading

Business & Leadership

- *The Servant Leader: Transforming Your Heart, Head, Hands and Habits* - Ken Blanchard & Phil Hodges
- *Great Leaders Grow: Becoming a Leader for Life* - Ken Blanchard & Mark Miller
- *Leadership by the Book: Tools to Transform Your Workplace* - Ken Blanchard, Bill Hybels and Phil Hodges
- *The One Minute Manager Builds High Performing Teams: Excellence Through Team Building* - Ken Blanchard, Donald Carew & Eunice Parisi-Carew
- *The 5 Levels of Leadership: Proven Steps to Maximize Your Potential* - John C. Maxwell
- *The 15 Invaluable Laws of Growth: Live Them and Reach Your Potential* - John C. Maxwell
- *The 21 Irrefutable Laws of Leadership: Follow Them and People Will Follow You* - John C. Maxwell
- *The 360 Leader: Developing Your Influence from Anywhere in the Organization* - John C. Maxwell
- *Leader Shift*: 11 Essential Changes Every Leader Must Embrace - John C. Maxwell
- *The Power of Ethical Management: Integrity Pays! You Don't have to Cheat to Win* - Kenneth Blanchard, Norman Vincent Peale
- *Raving Fans: A Revolutionary Approach to Customer Service* - Ken Blanchard, Sheldon Bowles

- *The Secret: What Great Leaders Know and Do* - Ken Blanchard, Mark Miller
- *Extraordinary Influence: How Great Leaders Bring Out the Best in Others* - Dr. Tim Irwin
- *Influence: The Psychology of Persuasion* - Robert Cialdini
- *Pre-Suasion: A Revolutionary Way to Influence and Persuade* - Robert Cialdini
- *How to Run Your Business by The Book: A Biblical Blueprint to Bless Your Business* - John C. Maxwell
- *Mastering a Serving Leader Attitude: Transform Yourself by Knowing, Controlling & Giving Yourself in New and Powerful Ways* - P. Griffith Lindell
- *The Compound Effect: Jumpstart Your Income, Your Life, Your Success* - Darren Hardy
- *Becoming a Coaching Leader: The Proven Strategy for Building Your Own Team of Champions* - Daniel Harkavy
- *Start With Why: How Great Leaders Inspire Everyone to Take Action* - Simon Sinek
- *Business by the Book: The Complete Guide of Biblical Principles for the Workplace* - Larry Burkett
- *The Starbucks Experience: The 5 Principles to Turning Ordinary into Extraordinary* - Joseph A. Michelli
- *The 4 Disciplines of Execution: Achieving your Wildly Important Goals* - Chris McChesney, Sean Covey, Jim Huling
- *Elon Musk: Tesla, SpaceX, and the Quest for a Fantastic Future* - Ashlee Vance

- *The Four: The Hidden DNA of Amazon, Apple, Facebook and Google* - Scott Galloway
- *The Go-Getter: The Classic Story That Tells You How to Be One* - Peter B. Kyne
- *Delivering Happiness: A Path to Profits, Passion and Purpose* - Tony Hsieh
- *Sticky Leadership: How Successful Entrepreneurs Get Their Leadership to Stick in the Heads, Hearts and Actions of Others* – Larry Briggs

Marketing and the Mind

- *Where's Your Wow?: 16 Ways to Make Your Competitors Wish They Were You!* - Robyn Spizman & Rick Frishman
- *The Face-to-Face Book: Why Real Relationships Rule in a Digital Marketplace* - Ed Keller & Brad Fay
- *How to Get Your Point Across in 30 Seconds or Less* - Milo O. Frank
- *The 22 Immutable Laws of Branding: How to Build a Product or Service into a World-Class Brand* - Al Ries & Laura Ries
- *Pendulum: How Past Generations Shape Our Present and Predict Our Future* - Roy H. Williams & Michael R. Drew
- *The Science of Likeability: 27 Studies to Master Charisma, Attract Friends, Captivate People and Take Advantage of Human Psychology* – Patrick King

- *Brain Rules: 12 Principles of Surviving & Thriving at Work, Home and School* - John Medina
- *The Influentials: One American in Ten Tells the Other Nine How to Vote, Where to Eat and What to Buy.* - Ed Keller & Jon Berry
- *Why We Buy: The Science of Shopping* - Paco Underhill
- *Purple Cow: Transform Your Business by Being Remarkable* - Seth Godin
- *Experiential Marketing: How to get Customers to Sense, Feel, Think, Act, Relate to your Company and Brands* - Bernd H. Schmitt
- *Platform Get Noticed in a Noisy World: A Step by Step Guide for Anyone with Something to Say or Sell* - Michael Hyatt
- *Outliers: The Story of Success* - Malcolm Gladwell
- *The Tipping Point: How Little Things Can Make a Big Difference* - Malcolm Gladwell
- *Relactional Leadership: When Relationships Collide with Transactions, Practical Tools for Every Leader* - Ford Taylor
- *Who Switched Off My Brain? Controlling Toxic Thoughts & Emotions* - Dr. Caroline Leaf
- *Switch on your Brain: The Key to Peak Happiness, Thinking and Health* - Dr. Caroline Leaf
- *Multipliers: How the Best Leaders Make Everyone Smarter* - Liz Wiseman
- *Contagious: Why Things Catch On* - Jonah Berger
- *Tribes: We Need You to Lead Us* - Seth Godin

- *The Power of Habit: Why We Do What We Do in Life and Business* - Charles Duhigg
- *Data-Driven Marketing: The 15 Metrics Everyone in Marketing Should Know* - Mark Jeffrey
- *Mindset: The New Psychology of Success* - Carol S. Dweck, Ph.D.
- *Do Your Children Believe? Becoming Intentional About Your Family's Faith and Spiritual Legacy* - Terence Chatmon
- *Measure What Matters: How Google, Bono, and the Gates Foundation Rock the World with OKR's* - John Doerr
- *Brain Myths Exploded: Lessons from Neuroscience* - Professor Indre Viskontas

Made in the USA
Las Vegas, NV
13 March 2023

69004526R00125